Outshine the Sun

40 Muslim Women in History

Written by
Abdul Rahman Latif

Illustrated by
H. Sumeyra Korkmaz

FONS VITAE

First published in 2024 by
Fons Vitae
49 Mockingbird Valley Drive
Louisville, KY 40207
http://www.fonsvitae.com
Email: fonsvitaeky@aol.com

Library of Congress Control Number: 2024930942
ISBN 978-1941610-947

Printed in South Korea

THIS WORK IS DEDICATED TO THE GRANDMOTHERS,
MOTHERS AND DAUGHTERS OF PALESTINE.

Chicago
Brooklyn
New York
Bermuda
Edinburg
Cordoba
Fez
Tripoli
Alexandria
Cairo
Istanbul
Kazan
Merv
Nishapur
Aleppo
Balkh
Yarkand
Baghdad
Tebnine
Kashgar
Basrah
Damascus
Karachi
Medinah
Kolkata
Delhi
Mecca
Touba
Sokoto
Zaria
Aceh
Johannesburg
40 MUSLIM WOMEN AROUND THE WORLD

Contents

In history and her-story,
We hear some tales of mystery.
We learn old truths and long-lost dreams,
We find these heroes of our deen.

These Forty Women changed the world-
They lived their faith and legends paled.
Their lights were brighter than the sun.
Let's read their stories one by one.

Khadijah bt. Khuwaylid

d. 619
Mecca, Saudi Arabia

The first convert to our new din,
The best support to al-Amin.
Of God's great grace, she is the proof;
Her love and strength are through the roof.

in her own words

When the Prophet ﷺ was overwhelmed after seeing angel Jibrail for the first time, when he asked her to cover him and expressed his worry, she responded to him with belief and hope. ***"Allah will never disgrace you,"*** she said, ***"for you treat your relatives well, speak the truth, help the poor and the needy, are generous to your guests, and aid those who have faced disasters."***

The illustration here depicts Khadijah with a large rose and several smaller buds. A rose, in traditional Sufi imagery, represents the Prophet ﷺ. The smaller buds represent the children that Khadijah رضي الله عنها and Rasul ﷺ had together: daughters Zaynab, Umm Kulthum, Ruqayya, and Fatima, and sons Abdullah and Qasim, both of whom passed away at a young age.

When the Prophet ﷺ felt alone, ***she provided him with company***. When he was in need, ***she supported him.*** And when he was hurt, ***she was a source of healing.***

Khadijah bt. Khuwaylid was the Prophet's ﷺ wife and ***the first person*** to believe in his message—and believe in him. When he was a young man, all promising prospects and no possessions, **she was an accomplished business woman.** She recognized his talent, and hired him. ***She proposed to him after being impressed by his good character, and they got married!***

Years later, when the Prophet ﷺ came down from the mountain after receiving the first words of Revelation, he was overwhelmed, confused and shivering. **Once again, she was a source of strength, gently covering him with a cloak and telling him that God would not mistreat him.** She testified to his honesty, stood by him when people laughed at the truth, *and persisted in faith despite facing rejection from her own people.*

After nearly twenty five years of true, caring companionship, she passed away. A little over a month later, the Prophet's uncle also died. The devastating feeling of loss the Prophet endured as a result marked this year as **"The Year of Sorrow."**

Long after her passing, the Prophet ﷺ would say of her, *"I was nurtured by her love."*

Lessons:

- Khadijah ﵂ trusted the Prophet ﷺ and recognized the truth. She was **a good judge of character**, but also did her best to **prove her beliefs and learn**. For example, she knew that Allah would not let the Prophet ﷺ be deceived, but still she took him to her cousin to discover that he was a Prophet.
- Khadijah ﵂ ***believed at a time when faith was strange and persecuted.*** Even when her livelihood was cut off, and the dismal situation drove her to her death, still her faith did not waver for a moment.

Fatima al-Zahra bt. Muhammad ﷺ

d. 632
Medinah,
Saudi Arabia

They dump filth on her father's back,
She cleans it off, she does not slack.
She cooks for neighbors through the night,
She gets her name due to her light.

in her own words:

One day Hasan رضي الله عنه, her son, noticed her praying for many believers but not for herself. He asked her about this, and she said, ***"My son! (Prioritize) neighbors first and our household next."***

In this illustration,
Fatima رضي الله عنها is dressed royally,
with skirts reaching out towards paradise
to represent her status as "the chief of all women of heaven."
The light around her face is an allusion to her nickname al-Zahrah, the radiant one.
The roses in her hand symbolize her children Hasan and Husayn رضي الله عنهما.

Scholars say that there have been over **50 BILLION** people who have lived on earth. Allah alone knows how many of those people will make it to paradise, but the number must be huge! The Prophet ﷺ once said that his daughter, ***Fatima, will be the chief of ALL the women of heaven.***

Fatima was the youngest daughter of the Prophet ﷺ and Khadijah bt. Khuwaylid. *When people tossed trash at her father while he prayed, she carefully cleaned it off him. Even when she was hungry, she would give up her share of food so others could eat.* She was noble and generous like her parents, a shining example in the history of our Ummah. It's appropriate then, that her nickname, al-Zahra, means "*the radiant one.*" Fatima married the courageous Ali; her children and grandchildren are some of the **most important** people in the entire history of Islam. ***It's not an exaggeration to say that her parenting skills changed the world!***

On one occasion, a group of Priests once challenged the Prophet ﷺ to a prayer contest—the Priests would pray and the Prophet ﷺ and a group of people he chose would also pray. The group who Allah favored would win. The Prophet ﷺ showed up to that prayer contest with ***Fatima, her husband Ali, and their two sons Hasan and Husayn.*** He covered them with his cloak, and when the Priests saw that blessed, holy family, they backed off.

Lessons:

- Fatima was a dutiful, loving daughter, mother, wife, and member of society. She was **caring and generous** in all her relationships, and those relationships impacted our whole history and faith!
- Fatima was a member of the family of the Prophet ﷺ. **The family of the Prophet ﷺ has historically been honored by Muslims around the world.** ***If you love someone, you love their family.*** *We love the Prophet ﷺ so we should remember and love his family too!* The duroods/salawat we typically

Ayesha bt. Abi Bakr

d. 678
Madinah, Saudi Arabia

She narrates what he said and did,
She stands her ground, she's never hid.
The Ummah's mother, scholar, guide-
They mocked her honor, God replied.

The illustration depicts how Ayesha ﷺ taught generations of scholars, who taught further generations until the present day, continuing the chain of knowledge from its source, the Prophet ﷺ, who is represented by a rose.

in her own words:

Ayesha ﷺ said,
"Ask Allah to help and give ease in everything, even if it's (tying) a shoelace. Because if Allah doesn't make it easy, it won't be possible."

When given a list of items, the average person can remember about 7 of them off the top of their head—give or take a couple. ***Ayesha ﷺ was not an average person.* She remembered hundreds of sayings and stories of the Prophet ﷺ, called hadith, word for word.**

She is one of the greatest narrators of hadith ever, and a huge chunk of our understanding of Islam comes through her!

Ayesha ﷺ was the daughter of the first Caliph Abu Bakr and the wife of the Prophet ﷺ. She was a curious and strong-willed child who grew into ***a confident, wise woman with unshakable faith.*** She spent her life preserving, living, and teaching what the Prophet ﷺ said and did. At one point during the Prophet's ﷺ life, people gossiped about her, and made up wicked lies about her character. **She remained strong in the face of the false accusations and trusted that Allah would take care of her.** And He did! Allah revealed verses of the Qur'an proving her innocence. After the Prophet ﷺ passed away, she became the de facto leader of the Mothers of the Believers (the Prophet's ﷺ wives), and was known for taking daring stances in her efforts to preserve our young ummah.

The Prophet ﷺ once said, "The superiority of Ayesha over other women is like the superiority of Tharid to other kinds of foods." Tharid must have been delicious!

Lessons:

- Ayesha ﷺ was a scholar who always shared what she knew. ***The pursuit of knowledge and spreading knowledge*** are major parts of our faith.
- Ayesha ﷺ was never shy when it came to **curiosity**!
- Ayesha ﷺ **trusted in Allah completely** and that trust always paid off.

Sumayyah bt. Khayyat

d. 615
Mecca, Saudi Arabia

The Sun burns hot, the sand is coal;
No matter what, her soul is whole.
The first one killed for holding fast,
God's grace, not pain, will always last.

In this illustration, Sumayyah is with her family, facing suffering with hope. Her heart is greater than her suffering, and it helps her cope with the hot sand.

Say it's 100 degrees out, and you absentmindedly touch the painted metal door of a car. ***Your hand burns at the touch, and you flinch, gingerly opening the door with raw, red fingers.*** You could probably cook an egg on the windshield.

Now imagine being wrapped in heavy metal, completely immobile, your skin becoming toasty. That's what happened to Sumayyah bt. Khayyat RA. She was one of the first converts to Islam, ***listed among the first seven to declare their faith in public.*** That was a risky, brave move considering she was a former slave occupying a dangerously low position in the wicked, pretentious Meccan society of Jahili/pre-Islamic times. She and her family were tortured for their acceptance of the faith—she was forced into hefty armor, and made to stand under the drooping desert sun. But no matter what was done to her—no matter the wounds she suffered, or the pain she felt, she never gave up on her faith, **not even for an instant**. **They could break her body but they could never break her will or her soul.**

The Prophet ﷺ once said, ***"Patience, O Family of Yasir (her husband). Truly, your meeting place will be in Paradise."*** Abu Jahl, the Prophet's ﷺ most adamant enemy, killed Sumayyah. **She was the first shahid, martyr, in Islam.** She went to paradise, and her husband reunited with her soon after. They were weak and hated in this world, but they are glorious and beloved in the next. Her son, Ammar, survived them and became one of the most distinguished companions of the Prophet ﷺ.

Lessons:

- If someone's life is in danger, they're allowed to hide the fact that they're Muslim. Sumayyah never did that though—she couldn't bear to live a lie even if it was okay. **She always stood for truth**. ***She lived and died for what she believed in.***
- Sumayyah رضي الله عنها suffered great hardship but she persisted in **patience** ***no matter what.***

exer

1. **Khadija رضي الله عنها comforted Rasul in some of his most difficult moments. Her presence itself was a source of peace for him.** Is there anyone in your life going through a difficult time? Brainstorm ways that you can give them comfort, and then put your ideas into practice! Maybe you can hug a friend, give them hot chocolate if its cold, talk to them, or even just sit with them? **Sometimes simply being there or asking how they are doing can make their day.** The Prophet ﷺ says that a smile is a charity! Even a kind glance can change someone's life.

2. **Fatima رضي الله عنها picked up the trash that was thrown on the Prophet ﷺ.** Harming and dirtying the Prophet ﷺ was an evil thing, but also polluting the environment and tossing trash on the ground in general is repugnant. ***If you see trash on the sidewalk, anywhere that its not supposed to be—pick it up!*** Use gloves if you can, and clean your hands afterwards. ***Maybe organize a trash clean up with your friends and family?***

3. **Fatima رضي الله عنها was often poor and hungry, but still she worked to feed those less fortunate than herself.** Feeding people's bellies is one of the most pure acts of charity. Look up whether there is a soup kitchen in your area. ***With your parents and friends, volunteer at the food kitchen and serve food like Fatima رضي الله عنها!***

cise

4 **Ayesha رضي الله عنها memorized and narrated thousands of Hadith!** *Try memorizing at least one. Here's a good one to start with. It was narrated by Ayesha رضي الله عنها herself!* [*Ayesha said:* **"I was on a camel that was acting difficult, and I started to hit it (so it would move). The Prophet ﷺ said, "*You have to be kind! Whenever there is kindness in something, it beautifies it. And whenever it's removed from something, it disgraces it.*"**]

5 **No matter how much she was hurt, Sumayyah رضي الله عنها held firm on her faith. What is something you can hold firm on that isn't easy?** *Is it doing your prayers, wearing a hijab, or maybe maintaining the pronunciation of your name? Whatever it is, whenever it gets tough, remember Sumayyah RA! Set a small goal first—praying just one more prayer, correcting people on how to say your name once every 5 times, whatever it is. When you've made it a regular practice, increase your goal until you're always living your faith to the fullest.*

6 **Note down a few times you avoided doing something good because you were afraid of other people judging you or being mean to you.** *Don't be hard on yourself, and always prioritize your safety, but write down what you think Sumayyah رضي الله عنها would have done in that circumstance.*

Nusaybah bt. Ka'b

d. 634
Madinah, Saudi Arabia

A nurse in battle, saving all,
She starts to see her people fall.
She will not see the Prophet hurt.
She grabs a bow and jumps, alert.

Even amid the fury of fighting, Nusaybah ﷺ thought to the far future. **"O messenger of Allah,"** she said, **"Ask Allah to make us your companions in paradise."** He prayed as she requested and she said with glee, **"After this, I do not care about whatever happens (next)."**

In this illustration, Nusaybah ﷺ fights, even when the odds are against her.

Nusaybah ﷺ was **one of the first converts** *from* Madinah. *She gave her pledge of allegiance* to the Prophet ﷺ directly, *and she lived up to it in her every word and deed.* She taught others the deen, *fought for it, and protected the* Messenger ﷺ during the **Battle of Uhud.**

On that day, battle raged on all sides—a storm of swords, arrows, screams, and chaos. The Muslims had been winning, the archers on the mountain of Uhud holding the Quraysh at bay. But after the archers abandoned their position, the situation reversed with a vengeance. ***Muslim forces fell to pieces like shattered glass.***

The Prophet ﷺ, **the beating heart of this young ummah,** was threatened. ***His blessed face bled.***
Nusaybah ﷺ was bringing water to the warriors and the wounded. When others ran from danger, she dashed to it. ***She scooped up a sword, plucked a bow and arrow, and put her body between the Prophet ﷺ and harm's way.***
She *fought fiercely, and* survived the battle with wounds but *also a* **smile**, *for the* Prophet ﷺ lived.

Lessons:

- Nusaybah *faced a* terrifying situation, and ***it wasn't her job to help.*** **But she did so anyway**, *because it was the right thing to do and because she loved the Prophet ﷺ!*
- Nusaybah ﷺ prioritized the hereafter over this life, and the safety of the Prophet over her own safety. **She had her priorities set towards transcendent heights.**

Zaynab bt. Ali

d. 682
Damascus, Syria

Oppression lies upon the land,
Her voice rings out, she takes a stand.
A martyred hero's memory lives
Because of lessons that she gives.

in her own words:

Knowing that status in this world and the next are two very different things, she said, ***"God spoke the truth, Yazid; 'Evildoers obtain to an evil end, for they reject God's signs and ridicule them.' Do you think that because we have been driven as captive slaves and forced to travel to the far reaches of the earth with no shelter but the sky, we are insignificant in God's eyes and you have honor?"***

In this illustration, Zaynab tells the story of the tragedy of karbala to the people, despite her imprisonment. She calls out the rulers and speaks Haqq—truth, which breaks the chain of injustice.

The Prophet ﷺ was once asked, "What is the best jihad?"
He answered, "A word of truth in front of an unjust ruler."

No one embodied this hadith more than his granddaughter, Zaynab RA. She spoke truth to power, and lived truth till her last hour. Yazid, the wanton, corrupt Caliph of her time, was a tyrant. Time and again, the people came to Zaynab's brother Husayn and asked him to rise up and fight on their behalf, to usher in an era of justice and a return to the values of the Prophet ﷺ. When he did so, traveling to the city of Kufa with a small contingent of followers, the people shamelessly abandoned him. Yazid's army surrounded his camp and cut them off from access to water.

What followed over the next ten days were some of the most tragic and sorrowful events of our entire history. Many members of the Prophet's ﷺ own family were murdered, and even an infant lost his precious life. Zaynab was one of the few survivors. ***She shielded her nephew, and though captive, told the story of what happened, keeping not only the memory of the tragedy but also its morals alive – always stand for justice and truth because it is right, not because you think you will succeed.*** When she was dragged before the tyrant Yazid, she did not cower or tremble. **She condemned the most dangerous man in the world without a tremor in her voice, for she feared Allah alone.**

Lessons:

- Zaynab رضي الله عنها **spoke truth to power**, ***and she condemned evil in every way possible.*** She lived up to the hadiths of her Grandfather the Prophet ﷺ about speaking a word of truth in front of an unjust ruler AND his statement that, ***"when you see an evil, change it with your hands, if you can't do that, speak out against it, and if you can't do that at least detest it in your heart."*** -Zaynab رضي الله عنها was imprisoned but she didn't let feelings of powerlessness stop her from raising awareness or making a difference.
- Zaynab رضي الله عنها defended her nephew even when she herself was in danger. **She did what she could to save the weak and protect family.**
- Zaynab رضي الله عنها used her eloquence and creativity in the pursuit of justice. ***She was a powerful speaker and storyteller and she used those skills in the cause of faith.***

Rabia Adawiyyah

d. 801
Basrah, Iraq

A famous roaming friend of God
Her actions might seem kind of odd.
She doesn't care for heaven, hell;
For love of God she acts so well.

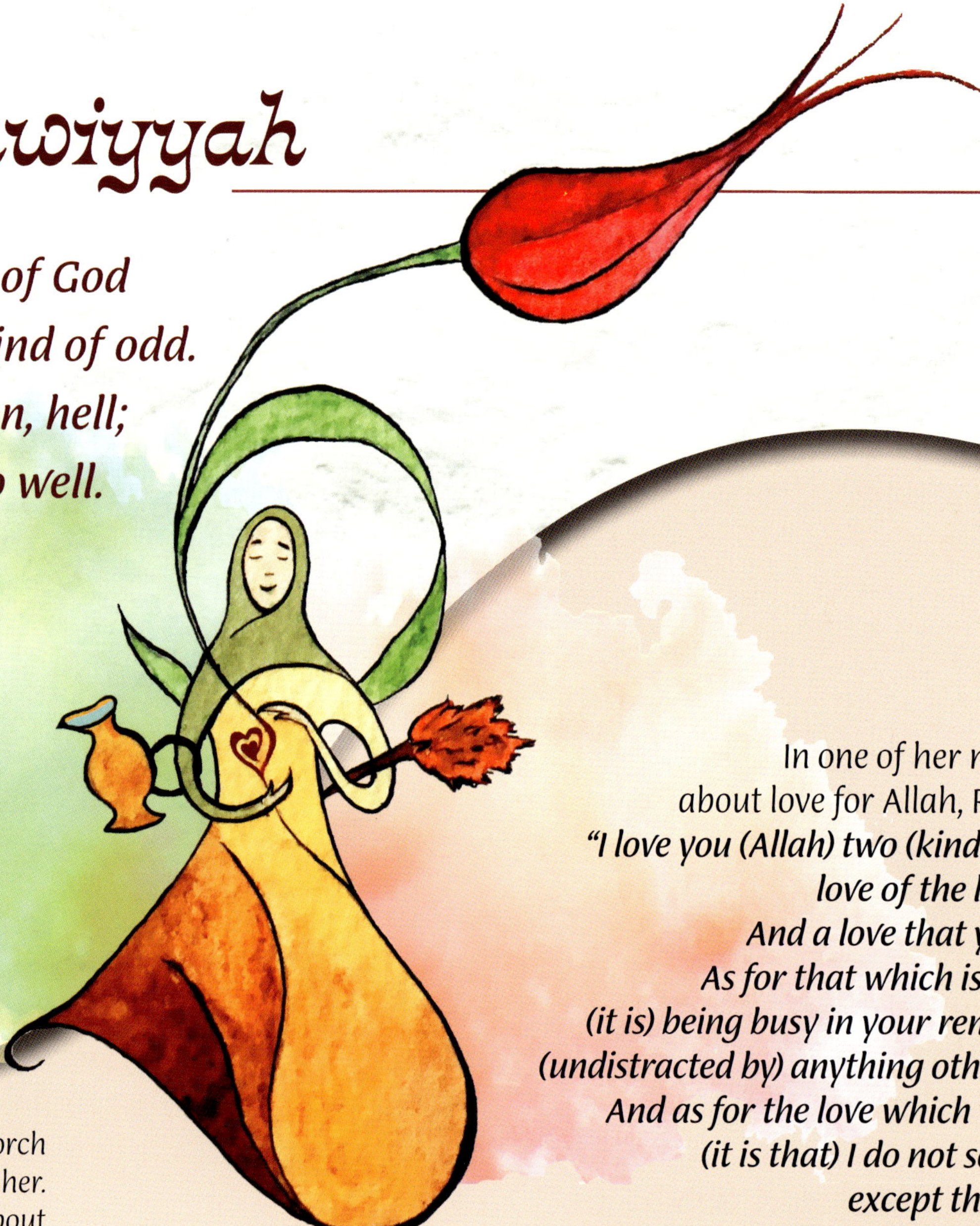

In one of her many poems about love for Allah, Rabia wrote,

"I love you (Allah) two (kinds of) loves—
love of the love for you,
And a love that you deserve.
As for that which is love of love
(it is) being busy in your remembrance,
(undistracted by) anything other than you
And as for the love which you deserve
(it is that) I do not see anything
except that I see you.
There is no praise in this or that for me
But there is praise for you in this and that."

The illustration depicts Rabia carrying a torch and bucket as in the famous story about her. Her double heart represents her poem about divine love, and the tulip is a common symbol to refer to Allah.

In the early life of the incredibly pious Rabia al-Adawiya, ***everything that could go wrong, went wrong.*** **Her parents were penniless.** Not even "poor as dirt," because one can at least grow things from the soil. And then her parents died; she went from having a family scraping to get by to ***no family at all.*** ***She was sold into slavery, as if being an orphan alone wasn't suffering enough.***And yet, through all the hardship and all the loss, **she prayed**. Her master walked by one night as she was worshiping, ***and he probably lost his balance upon seeing her***. ***An otherworldly light glowed above her head.*** He let her go—whether in fear, awe, or repentance, we do not know. Rabia was destined to have ***no master but Allah.***

She wandered the land, her every thought and every act concerned about God. **The greatest scholars and spiritual seekers of her time sought her out, to learn from her, like children at her feet.** There are numerous stories about her words and actions; some are fanciful but all are profound. **It is said that one day she walked around carrying a flaming torch and a bucket of cool water.** When asked what she was doing with them, she answered that she wanted to burn down heaven with the torch and put out the fires of hell with the water, **because she wished for people to do good not in fear of punishment or hope for a reward, but for the love of Allah alone.**

Lessons:

- ***Love of Allah*** **was everything for Rabia al-Adawiyah**. It was the supreme concern of her life, and far beyond just saying she loved Allah, ***she spent every moment thinking about him, serving him, and worshiping him.***
- Rabia al-Adawiyah **didn't care what people thought about her and never tried to show off for them, but still became famous and people came from far and wide to learn from her.** She didn't care about this world, or even about the hereafter, but only about Allah. **People become close to what they care most about.**

Ulayya bt. Al-Mahdi

d. 801
Basrah, Iraq

In front of family she sings,
Her lines leap up and soar with wings.
She reads Qur'an and history,
Her life a pious mystery.

In one of her poems
Ulayya wrote and sang,
"Ease my stress a little,
For I have become so thin/
Do for me beautiful things,
To make my mind spin."
Her story and words continue
to make minds spin today.

In this illustration, Ulayya sings in the palace garden while her brothers play instruments and the birds revel in the tune.

Imagine being the daughter of a doting king and the beloved younger sister of another. *Life is easy, life is bliss.* ***Every enjoyment possible is at your fingertips.***

Ulayya was born into the exact situation of royal ease. ***However, rather than just party and have fun, she chose to pray, write... and perform.*** Rather than just enjoy beautiful things, ***she wrote beauty into existence.*** Her piety and her poetic skill together made her name and talent travel well-beyond the royal palace of the Abbasids.

She trained other musicians and composed **over 70 songs by herself**. She played with ideas in traditional poetry, pulling off new twists—for example replacing the desert featured in bedouin poetry with a garden. Some of her poems are about love, some speak of familial devotion, and others are silly, ***but all are beautiful products of an artistic genius.***

Lessons:

-Ulayya **strove for excellence**, and she made sure others would benefit from that hard work. ***She worked hard in her musical composition, and the whole world was enriched.*** She had a talent and she didn't let it go to waste.

-Ulayya was engaged in her time's equivalent of the '**entertainment industry,**' ***but she always kept things halal.*** Her poems were about clean topics and her comportment was admirable. That didn't make her work dull though—it was more a foundation than a restriction for her music.

exer

1 **Nusaybah ﵂ physically defended the Prophet ﷺ.** *How can you protect the Prophet and his legacy today? How about with your words and good behavior?* Write a few sentences defending the Prophet ﷺ.

2 **Nusaybah ﵂ literally jumped in front of the Prophet and blocked the path of his enemies.** When you're the goalie or a defender in soccer, when you block the path of the groom in a south Asian wedding, or when you defend someone else in dodgeball, you're making the same bodily motions she was. Try and think about her in those circumstances!

3 **When you see someone getting hurt, or being attacked—protect them!** It doesn't matter who they are. If someone is being physically attacked, call an adult—don't get into a fight yourself. If someone is saying something mean to someone else, speak up!

4 **What tragedies are occuring today? How can you be a Zaynab for the victims?** The plight of the Rohingya, the Uyghurs, the people of Palestine, of so many others around the world, mimics that of the heroic martyrs of Karbala. Do research into one situation of Muslims being persecuted today. ***Tell your friends about what you learned and maybe do a project on it for school!*** Then save pocket money and donate to a fundraiser with your parents. It doesn't matter if its a small amount, it's the intention that counts!

5 **Learn about the story of Imam Husayn and the tragedy at Karbala which Zaynab ﵂ worked so hard to convey.** It has been told, retold, and commemorated by Muslims of all backgrounds for centuries. It's a painful story to hear, but Zaynab ﵂ trusted us to listen.

cise

6 **Rabia remembered Allah with her every breath.** Dhikr is the word used for remembrance and it also refers to the practice of repeating phrases glorifying Allah. Try doing dhikr! **Start with what was probably Rabia's favorite Dhikr—say La Illaha Illa Allah (there is no God but God) 100 times!**

7 **Rabia saw the divine everywhere.** Write down instances in life where you feel and see Allah's presence. Then write down instances where you don't,. **What is the difference between the two types of incidents?** Ponder how Allah is present in each of those moment's where you don't immedietly think of him. E.g. He made you exist in those moments, he created the environemnt you are in, etc.

8 Loving God starts with treating his creation with love too. **Tell your family and friends that you love them!**

9 Write down all the things you can think of that you enjoy doing! It couldw be anything—watching TV, listening to music, or taking hikes. It could even be reading hadiths or history books. With each of them, ask yourself if the content is wholesome and halal. If it isn't, ask yourself how you can find better alternatives.

10 Pick a Nasheed or Naat—a song praising Allah or the Prophet ﷺ, and sing it with your family! ***It's okay if everyone is off-tune, just make sure to enjoy it!***

Fatima Nishapuri

d. 838
Balkh, Afghanistan & Nishapur, Iran

She leads her students on the path
To love of God and not His wrath.
She knows a truth that is so deep,
The price it costs—this world—is cheap.

"
in her own words

When her to-be husband Ahmad hesitated to do the right thing, Fatima confronted him confidently, enjoing good and forbidding evil, and encouraging him to be who he aspired to be and not just who he was. ***"Be a guide! Not a highwayman (robber)!"*** she said.

In this illustration, Fatima literally gives up the world for the sake of divine love, and teaches her students to do the same. The sparkling path that she sits on represents the path to closeness to the divine.

Fatima was the daughter of the governor of the storied city of *Balkh.* ***She was a woman of wealth and power.* She gave it all up without a second thought** to live a life of quiet reflection, for she knew that true riches rest in learning about God.

Fatima moved to Nishapur with her husband Ahmed, who was a mystic. One day Ahmed wanted to put together *a spectacular welcoming party* for another mystic coming to the city. He asked Fatima for her advice, unsure how to proceed. She began listing the number of animals they would need to feed the people. When she mentioned preparing extra food, beyond what would feed everyone, he stopped her in confusion. "When a nobleman comes to dine," she explained, "**the dogs of the neighborhood must get a share of the feast too."** **She was so generous she would feed animals while others thought of feasting.**

Fatima taught some of the greatest spiritual masters of her time, including the legendary Dhu'-Nun al-Misri and unique Bayezid Bistami. The latter said, ***"In all my life, I have only seen one true man and one true woman. That woman was Fatima of Nishapur. There was no station (on the spiritual path) about which I spoke with her, but that she had already experienced it herself."***

Lessons:

- Fatima of Nishapur dedicated her life to **contemplating the divine,** and ***did not make her wealth or possessions her focus.*** She didn't care about leaving a fancy privileged life and looked for spiritual wealth in others, not material riches.
- Even when Fatima didn't have that much, still she wanted to make sure everyone was fed, even the animals. **She wasn't picky in who she was charitable to.** ***The Prophet ﷺ was a Mercy to all mankind and all creation.*** She tried to follow that example as much as possible.

Fatima al-Fihri

d. 880
Fez, Morocco

She builds for knowledge and its worth,
The oldest college on the earth.
She goes and works at any cost,
To make sure Wisdom won't be lost.

In this illustration, Fatima stands before the university she sponsored. The candle lamp at the gate represents the light of knowledge. The tile work design is in the shape of the city of Fez.

The Prophet ﷺ once said, "***The best charity is when a Muslim gains knowledge, and teaches it to his brother.***" What kind of charity, then, is building **an entire school**—***one which has been a center of learning and teaching knowledge for almost 1200 years?***

Fatima was from the influential Tunisian al-Fihri family, which moved to the city of Fez, in Morocco. ***She spent her inheritance to found al-Qarawiyyin—a school and mosque with one of the most fantastic libraries in the world.*** It quickly became the top institution of higher learning in the region and **one of the greatest centers of knowledge in the world.** *One might call it the "Harvard" of North Africa,* except it's nearly 800 years older than its Ivy league copycat. In fact, depending on how the term is defined, al-Qarawiyyin is the oldest constantly active 'college' on earth. Even centuries after its founding, it remained an elite center of higher learning. Several non-Muslims also chose to study there, such as the famed Jewish philosopher Maimonides.

Lessons:

- **Pursuing knowledge** "even all the way to China" is a central Muslim value. ***Helping others in their pursuit of knowledge*** is incredibly valuable in the site of Allah. **Fatima is THE role model in this regard.**
- An old saying goes that ***if you give someone a fish, you'll feed them for a day, but if you teach someone to fish, you'll feed them for their whole life***. Fatima went a step further than this—she created an institution where large numbers of people were taught, and many of them became teachers too—they could 'feed others' and not just themselves. Fatima thought about the long term when it came to education. It's just a metaphor, ***but dang that's a lot of fish.***

Rabia al-Balkhi

d. 10th century
Balkh, Afghanistan

The persian language tastes so sweet
She drinks its words, a sherbet treat.
Her life is marked by love and loss,
But still her poems shine like gloss.

"

In one couplet, she writes about the themes of love so important in her work, ***"O wind of sleeplessness, take my message to the beloved/ Tell that fair moon, 'Bring together the heart and soul."***

In the illustration, Rabia is depicted 'cooking up' her poetry. Her couplet about the wind of sleeplessness is written in Persian in the pot.

Rabia was born with ***the soul of a poet—and the skill to match.*** Growing up in the ancient city of **Balkh** in Afghanistan, **she saw the world with wonder, looking with her soul and not just her eyes.** She wrote of deep, true love and its many forms, in elegant verses. She became ***the first female poet*** in post-7th century Persian, a language famous for its poetic nature and rich literature.

Though her heart was open, the world can at times be closed. Her tyrannical brother sneered at her love for a slave, probably angry that a member of his mighty elite family might marry someone so 'lowly.' He caged his own sister—***but her words flew free,*** from the 10th century to the 21st. Several buildings are named after her in Afghanistan, including a hospital in Kabul, and she was the subject of the first Afghani feature film.

Lessons:

- Islam is a religion that begins with revelation—with the divine word. It makes sense that *our entire civilization celebrates beautiful words,* whether they are poems or books. Rabia al-Balkhi followed it in that tradition of exploring the possibilities of language with a unique vigor.
- **Words do matter, *and they can make a difference.*** Rabia al-Balkhi was oppressed by her own sibling, but her words were so powerful that almost no one remembers her brother, ***but everyone remembers what she said.***

Lubna de Córdoba

d. 10th century
Cordoba, Spain

A great old mathematics whiz,
Who knows what real life magic is.
A scribe of two new caliphs' courts,
more noble than all in their forts.

In this illustration, Lubna is working with arabic numerals and geometric tools. The arch is modeled after the fabled arches of the Mezquita de Córdoba, and the Arabic phrase under it is an Andalusian slogan especially associated with the Nasrid dynasty—"There is no victor except Allah."

There is a lot we don't know. We don't know exactly how light works, or whether the universe is made up of strings or dots. **We don't know what tomorrow holds, and a lot of the past is fuzzy too.** We don't know if Lubna de Cordoba was a scribe or a librarian for the Caliph, or if she was a freed slave or immigrant worker. What we do know is that she is someone ***who always wanted to know,*** to fill that endless gap in knowledge which plagues and enchants humanity.

She was the most famous **among the many Andalusian women active in scholarly activities at the time.** One biographer wrote two centuries after Lubna's death that she was ***"an intelligent writer, grammarian, poetess, (who was) knowledgeable in arithmetic, (and) comprehensive in her learning; no one in the palace was as noble as her..."***

Lessons:

- There were far more women doing amazing things in the past than we know about—unfortunately many records didn't survive, **and often women just weren't written about.** That is changing now, ***and it needs to continue to change.*** Despite the little that has been written about her, Lubna's education and brilliance still stands out. **She's another example of the importance of pursuing knowledge—not just in religion though, but in science, math, etc too!**
- *Muslims basically invented math, and Lubna was a part of that effort.* ***The word algebra comes from Arabic, and the word algorithm comes from the name of the guy who invented algebra.*** Men and women both were involved in math and science. Today there is a big gender gap in the **"STEM"** fields—***science, technology, engineering, and math.*** **Muslim women should be dominating these fields like Lubna and inshaallah they will!**

exer

1 Do you have a pet? Do you have a friend who has a pet? Or is there a cat or another animal that lives on the streets near you? Tell your parents, and together leave some food for the animal. **Do what Fatima did and be generous to all creation.**

2 Fatima thought a lot about God—now you try doing the same! **For 10 minutes, do nothing but think about God, about how great God is, how much he loves you and cares for all creation**. Think about the particular blessings you've received, and how even in difficulty he is there. Think about all the traits and names of God that you can. You can sit while you do this, or lie down, or close your eyes, whatever you want—but only think about God.

3 Fatima al-Fihri founded an incredible school that combined the study of Islam with the whole world. What would your own ideal school look like? Draw it! List the subjects that are studied there, and think about how you can increase your own skills in those subjects!

4 Fatima was all about learning and teaching! Write down something you know that other people around you don't know. Is it a fact about Islam? Does it increase people's sense of wonder? Teach three people about that thing in a polite and patient manner. Did you enjoy teaching?

5 Rabia al-Balkhi might have been the first female poet in Persian, but she wasn't the last! There were Muslim poets before her in Arabic, and there were so many after her. **Muslims have always loved poetry, and even the Prophet ﷺ enjoyed the occasional verse. For centuries, the mark of an educated**

cise

Muslim was that they wrote poetry—even if it wasn't good. Try writing your own poem! Start with a couplet—that a two line poem which rhymes. It doesn't have to be anything fancy, and the theme could be about anything—love of God, your family, the weather, that really cute cat. And don't stop there—write more!

6 **Whats a topic you don't know anything about, but you want to learn about? Right the topic down.** How would Lubna approach something she doesn't know? Try doing some 'research'! Get your parents or teacher to help you look up information about the topic. Check out the library, or use a search engine. Write a paragraph about what you've learned, and what you want to know next. **Its important that this research isn't for school but is because YOU want to learn.**

7 Lubna studied so many different subjects. You might not enjoy every subject you have to learn for school and life. **What's a subject that you're struggling with right now?** Draw Lubna trying to learn that subject, think about how she might approach it, and then do your best.

8 **Think about how you can promote Muslim women's participation in STEM fields—science, technology, engineering, and math, both where you live and abroad!** Maybe you can study those fields but of course we need people who are experts in everything so don't feel pressured. With your parents' help, look up events raising awareness about Women in Stem—promote those events and attend them!

al-Ijliyah al-Asturlabi

d. 10th century
Aleppo, Syria

One cloudless night she stares at stars,
She squints real hard to find red Mars.
So where do all the bright dots go?
She does the math so she can know.

In this illustration, al-Ijliyah gazes at the stars while resting on the crescent moon.

What do asteroid 7060 and the science fiction book Binti have in common? ***They're both connected to al-Ijliyah al-Asturlabi,*** **scientist and technician extraordinaire.** ***Asteroid 7060 is named al-Ijliyah in her honor, and the book Binti features a fictional version of her as the main character.***

Al-Ijliyah was from a Syrian family of Astrolabe makers—the 'al-asturlabi' part of her name refers to this. **Astrolabes are devices used to calculate the positions and movements of the stars and planets.** Her teacher was the maker of ***the oldest*** surviving astrolabe in the world. Al-Ijliyah was employed by the court of Sultan Sayf al-Dawla to make the night sky more easy to understand and map.

Many medieval Muslims like al-Ijlliyah were obsessed with astronomy, in part for practical reasons like figuring out the direction for prayer, and in part for spiritual reasons like following the Quranic commands to think about the heavens. **Like the celestial objects she studied, al-Ijliyah was a star.**

Lessons:

- Allah's revelation is the Qur'an, but in a sense, **so is the natural world.** ***The whole universe is filled with Allah's signs.*** Contemplation of the natural world—of the valleys, the trees, and the skies, is a part of our faith and an act of worship. al-Ijlliyah was probably a great worshiper of God—**she didn't just contemplate the natural world, she made its numerical wonders apparent.**
- al-Ijliyah didn't just use astrolabes, it seems that **she made them too. She was a scientist and an engineer.** Like Lubna, she was a great example of a historical Muslim woman involved in the stem field. She followed a quranic command **AND scientific curiosity, without contradiction.**

Karima al-Marwaziyya

d. 1070 | Merv, Turkmenistan
& Mecca, Saudi Arabia

Our books are wisdom, every page,
She makes them grace the center stage.
All students travel far and roam,
To study in her simple home.

Al-Dhahabi recounts that a young scholar wanted to check his own copy of hadith accounts against her version by comparing the texts by himself. She said, ***"No. Rather, check the texts together with me."*** She was concerned with accuracy and with guiding her students.

In this illustration, Karima is teaching students hadith. Chains of roses represent the isnads—chains of transmission—which link her students to her, and link her to the Prophet ﷺ.

If you ever look at a hadith in a hadith book, you'll notice a list of names at the start of the texts—*'so and so narrated from so and so who narrated from so and so...'* -**until you get to the Prophet ﷺ.** This chain of transmission, called an **isnad**, is a crucial part of the hadith which ***provides evidence that the account is authentic.*** **The isnad showcases a direct, unbroken connection to Muhammad ﷺ.** Someone with an 'ijaza' in a hadith, is part of a living breathing chain going back directly to the start of our religion.

Karima was ***a famous hadith scholar*** known for her mastery and transmission of ***Sahih Bukhari,*** perhaps ***the most significant book documenting accounts of the Prophet ﷺ ever.*** Karima was from the region around the famed silk road city of **Merv** in what is now Turkmenistan. She moved to **Mecca** and lived a pious life devoted to learning and teaching. ***Students came from as far away as Spain and Iraq to study with her,*** **and to link themselves to the words of the Prophet ﷺ through her.** She set up reading sessions where students recited hadiths they recorded, and she corrected them as necessary. **40** students transmitted individual hadith or the whole of *Sahih Bukhari* based on her authority. Each of them would have transmitted hadiths to others, who would have transmitted to others... ***The number of chains Karima features in must be enormous.***

Lessons:

- Karīma lived at a time distant from the Prophet ﷺ but she was still connected with him—not just by her love, **but through an actual chain of people through history! We can also be connected in both ways too.**
- The verification of chains of transmission was important to Karīma. **Authenticity and accuracy** were values she carried with her and exemplified, ***in both her scholarly work and faith.***

Wallada bt. al-Mustakfi

d. 1091
Cordoba, Spain

Her court is like a book salon,
With rhyming class in its diwan.
She paints a picture with her words,
And gardens grow, all filled with birds.

In this illustration, Wallada is depicted writing poetry and running a literary salon. Her poem about when the night falls is written in gold, while her famous boast is written on her sleeve. In the background, the legendary gardens of her home, Andalucia, are visible.

Wallada was full of it. *Prideful, boastful, a whole boatload of qualities we definitely shouldn't copy.* But, the truth is, her **confidence** was totally justified. She was as good as she said—and probably better. ***Her beautiful, bewildering, and sometimes biting verses are still the most-well known pieces of Andalusian poetry.*** Though Wallada was the daughter of a short-lived Caliph of Muslim Spain, she earned her reputation ***all by herself.*** She hosted **some of the greatest literary gatherings of her day**, and **dueled one of Andalusia's other superstar poets, Ibn Zaydun**, *in the medieval equivalent of rap battles.* **She won with every sharp verse.**

In one of her poems, Walada writes, ***"Expect me when night falls, For I see that the night best conceals our secrets /My love for you is such that if stars were to feel it, The sun would not shine and the moon would not rise, nor would the stars undertake their nocturnal journey."*** In another famous couplet, she boasts, ***"I am fit for high positions—by God/ And I am going my way with pride."***

Lessons:

- Wallada was a **poetic genius.** Like Ulayya, she worked to perfect her craft and make herself the best. ***Striving for excellence is a major value in our Religion, and Wallada was certainly excellent.***
- **Giving and receiving criticism** is really important, and that's exactly what Wallada would have done in her literary circle. The Prophet ﷺ said that faith is advice/constructive critique. ***When giving a critique, remember that your words and your intentions should be focused on making the other person better and not putting them down. When receiving a critique, try to look at yourself objectively, and see how you can improve based on it, but don't get caught up in feeling down about it.*** **We are all on a journey to improve ourselves!**

Razia Sultana

d. 1240
Delhi, India

Above her brothers she now stands,
She knows that time is shifting sands.
The people push for her to rule,
As she was just and never cruel.

In this illustration, Razia Sultan is depicted in her full royal splendor seated on an Elephant! The elephant's trunk hold's scales which represent her commitment to justice and flowers which represent her desire to nurture her people.

A wizened old warrior-king looked fondly upon his children. His sons were irresponsible and pompous, but his daughter was a bright spot in his life, and his hope for the future. When the end came, the Sultan of Delhi, Iltutmish, wished for princess Razia to take the throne. Corrupt nobles plotted, and a foolish brother became boss instead. He did worse than his father could have imagined, spending time on his own pleasures rather than the peoples' interests.

Razia stepped in to clean up her brother's mess. *She ruled with both strength and justice, mercy and might.* ***She rode before the people on an enormous elephant in a royal display of glory.*** Those supporters who thought they could manipulate her and pull strings from behind the scenes, were sorely disappointed. They tried again to cheat her out of her birth right, and succeeded. She scrambled to regain the throne, but lost her life in the attempt.

The medieval historian Juzjani writes, ***"(Razia was) a great king, with intelligence and wisdom, who enacted justice on the Earth, nurtured the people and the army, and in all (ways) possessed every quality that a king possessed."***

Lessons:

- Razia didn't wait for someone else to come along and solve all her people's problems. She knew she was qualified, and she stepped up to the plate. **She didn't tolerate incompetence or corruption, and led by example.**
- Even though Razia's reign was short, and its end was not what she would have wanted, it's the fact that she did right which matters. *As Muslims we are supposed to do good, regardless of the end result.*

exer

1 **Go stargazing!** If you live in a rural area, you can probably see the stars from your window. If you live in the big city, you might not be able to. Make a plan with your parents and maybe also your friends and their families too! Use 'dark sky maps,' to determine areas nearby where the stars are really truely visible. Then, on a night when there are no clouds, and there is no moon, travel together to star gaze! Draw the constellations that you see. Did you spot the milky way? Remember to think about the magnificence of Allah's universe and recite the verse of the Qur'an 6:97 ***"And it is He (Allah) who placed for you the stars that you may be guided by them through the darkness of the land and sea. We have detailed the signs for a people who know."***

2 **Have you ever seen an astrolabe before?** Make a trip to a history museum and find one! How do you think it was used? Doesn't it look complicated?

3 Karīma was a master of hadith, so It's time to memorize another Hadith! This was the first hadith that most teachers (probably including Karīma) would teach their students and it's utterly beautiful. Abdullah ibn Amr reported: The Messenger of Allah, peace and blessings be upon him, said, ***"The merciful will be shown mercy by the Most Merciful. Be merciful to those on the earth and the One in the heavens will have mercy upon you."***

4 **Karīma was a master of Isnads—chains of transmission.** Chains of transmission are a technique common throughout Islamic sciences, not just hadith! Why don't you practice a chain of transmission of good deeds to get a sense of how these chains work. Give a candy to a friend of yours, and tell her she has to give a candy to a friend of hers and tell that friend to give one to someone else, and so one. At each point, the one who gives a candy has to tell whoever came before them in the chain who they're giving a candy to. Record all the names. How far did you get before people stopped reporting back or you lost track?

cise

5 You wrote a couplet after reading the biography of Rabia al-Balkhi. **Try writing another poem—but this time don't stop there! Find at least one other friend, and get her to write a poem too.** Then share your poems with each other, discuss what you like about their poem, and what they can improve on. Congratulations—you've created your very own 'literary salon.' If you really want to channel Wallada, work with a friend to do a poetry duet! Write a poem to your friend and have your friend write one in response!

6 Wallada recognized her own good qualities and had super self-confidence. Humility and humbleness are very important in Islam, but they are different from putting yourself down. **Think for a while, and write down a few things you are good at.** Rather than just take pride in them, thank Allah for them and remember they wouldn't be possible without him, say Mashaallah, and don't brag—but be confident!

7 **If you were the ruler of your country like Razia was the Sultana of hers, what would you do?** How would you make society more just? How would you help the people? Write down your plans!

8 **What's a time you did something good but it didn't work out how you wanted it to?** What would you have done differently? What lessons can you learn from the incident and how can Razia's example and the idea that worldly success doesn't matter as much as action and intention inform your understanding of the situation?

Shajar al-Durr

d. 1257
Cairo, Egypt

She starts her life a humble girl,
This star of epics, tree of pearls.
She sees the French crusaders' end,
Her reign is short, but marks a mend.

According to Sirat al-Zahir Baibars,
when Shajar al-Durr received control of Egypt she said,
"I will praise my lord every hour/
for the bounty which I cannot exhaust.
The Generous has granted me his favor/
My wishes have reached me from the world
The lord of humankind has honored me with His glory/
and given me a gift which I am not equal to.
For Him is praise, thanks and grace/
For giving to me Egypt and what is in it"

In this Illustration, Shajar al-Durr is seated before a flower with pearls on the petals, referencing the meaning of her name. In the background is Cairo and Giza.

Farmers don't normally pull magic swords from stones and become kings, and serving girls don't usually find fairy godmothers and transform into princesses. Rags to riches stories sound fantastic, but too often they're fiction. But not always. Allah can change the state of anyone at any moment, and He certainly changed the circumstances of Shajar al-Durr—though she always acted regal. Shajar al-Durr, whose name means "Tree of Pearls," was a slave who became Sultan. She was the wife of the last Ayyubid Sultan whose dynasty descended from Saladin and his family. When her husband died she took power. She reigned during the chaotic transition period between two governments. Her soldiers crushed the Crusaders in Egypt and she sponsored some fancy architecture in the region—including the Salihiyya Madrassa—which her husband also contributed to—and her own mausoleum.

There were daggers at her throat and enemies in every shadow, but Shajar al-Durr thrived amid the political intrigue and gave as good as she got until the very end. Her legacy was immortalized in the folk epic Sirat al-Zahir Baibars.

Lessons:

- Shajar al-Durr came from an incredibly humble background, but she still rose to the greatest heights. Allah can literally change the situation of anyone—there is nothing that cannot be accomplished if He so wills it.
- Shajar al-Durr ruled during a chaotic time, but rather than just focus on survival, she tried to protect the people and build for the future. She made the best of difficult circumstances.
- In the folklore version of Shajar al-Durr she is super ambitious. If you know that you can help and do things better than they are being done, don't let shyness or humility stop you from acting—Shajar al-Durr didn't. In folklore, Shajar al-Durr is also very grateful to Allah for what she has received. Ambition is fantastic when it's grounded in gratitude.

Queen Amina of Zaria

d. 15th or 16th century
Zaria, Nigeria

The roads are long and scary too;
She makes them safe like morning dew.
This mighty empress conquers lands,
And builds them up with her own hands.

In this illustration, Queen Amina holds a staff, ready to defend her lands. The flowing fabric represents the many roads she built.

A woman rode on horseback, a sword in one hand, a raised fist in the other, and a legion of 20,000 troops marching and galloping behind her. "AllahuAkbar! Allah is the Greatest!" She yelled ferociously as she charged forward. She leaned in towards her mount's ears before she reached the enemy, and whispered the kalima "There is no god but Allah," just in case the hero and her horse fell in the coming fight. The sea of soldiers cried out the name of their beloved queen as they rushed to join her, their roar rising above the din of hundreds of hooves and the clattering of steel. "Queen Amina!" "For Zazzau!"

Amina was the warrior queen of Zazzau, now Zaria in modern-day Nigeria. There is no sugar-coating it—she spent her career waging war, and won. Stories say she led her forces herself, riding on horseback into the field ahead, though the details might not be exactly like the fictional version above. *She became a living legend.* But despite all the glory and all the love of her people, ***greed and ego were never her motivators, and praise and wealth were never her goals.*** She secured the roads around her kingdom through her conquests, thereby protecting merchants from attacks, and securing the prosperity of her people. She is said to have built walls to defend her city, introduced a new plant for farming in the region, and promoted a new, more effective type of armor. This powerful ruler and innovator is honored in the ***Kano Chronicle***, a history of the Hausa people of Nigeria, where it writes: ***"At this time Zaria, under Queen Amina, conquered all the towns as far as Kworarafa and Nupe. Every town paid tribute to her...In her time the whole of the products of the west were brought to Hausaland. Her conquests extended over thirty-four years."***

Lessons:

- Queen Amina had to do a lot of things that were difficult and definitely not fun. Fighting, risking her life constantly—it had to be nerve-wracking. But because her ultimate goal was great, she kept on going no matter what.

Queen Amina didn't just defend her people—she did so in inventive ways! Her rule was marked by **cleverness and new ideas.** ***Simply having a noble goal and working towards it isn't everything—figuring out the best way to accomplish it is ihsan, pursuing perfection and goodness.***

A'isha al-Ba'uniyya

d. 1517
Damascus, Syria & Cairo, Egypt

Prolific means she does a lot;
She writes so much, her pen is hot!
She masters knowledge and her nafs,
This life alone is not enough.

In this illustration, A'isha is depicted holding one of her children. This is in reference to her commitment to scholarship while raising a family. The large scroll represents her many books, the roses symbolize her writing about the Prophet ﷺ, and the tulips signify her treatises about God. Her journey to Egypt is also portrayed.

How much can you write in an hour? A page? Half a page? How long would it take you to write a whole book? Or how about 10 whole books, all written with elegant wording and intelligent ideas.
A'isha al-Ba'uniyya composed over 20 works, the most of any woman in Arabic before the 18th century. Every work touched on the inner workings of faith in a different way. She composed a ***mawlid***, a text celebrating the birth and life of the Prophet ﷺ, and wrote a magnificent expansion of the ***Burdah***, the most recited poem in the world which praises the Prophet.

She also raised two kids while at the peak of her scholarly career. Her life, like her scholarship, was never static or stagnant. ***Rather than coop up in a library, she traveled to seek knowledge, exchanging quips and ideas with Egypt's most illustrious figures.***

A'isha wrote, ***"Know, may God show you mercy, that love is God's most wondrous secret. It is the result of being chosen, the effect of designation, the means to proximity, and the ascension to union. Love is pure grace, pure generosity, and true munificence..."*** A'isha knew that secret very well.

Lessons:

- A'isha kept at her scholarship and writing for her whole life. **20 books weren't written in a day.** She worked hard, she worked for a long time—and **she constantly expanded her creative and intellectual horizons,** carrying the same themes of God's love and devotion into new genres of writing.
- A'isha **raised children while still being a scholarly powerhouse!** People may say that one has to choose between education and family, or work and family, but A'isha shows that with hardwork and dedication, doing both is very much a possibility! If anything, her writing was enhanced by her family life. For example, she had given birth before, so who better than her to write about the birth of the Prophet

Amannisa Khan

d. 1560
Yarkand, China-Occupied East Turkestan

Her songs stop hearts and make her queen,
Her efforts paint the whole land green.
"The twelve Muqams" she hears and writes,
They sound to us like many lights.

According to the biographer Mu'jiz, when the Sultan doubted Amannisa's poetical powers he said "Here, let me watch while you write a poem." Mujiz writes, "The girl got out her ink holder, pen, and paper and wrote (as part of the poem): ***'Oh Lord, this slave [meaning 'Abd ar-Rashīd] has strange suspicions of me, As if this evening in this house a thorn grew into me.*** The Sultān laughed and said, 'I am convinced. Don't make fun of me.'"

In this illustration Amannisa Khan is depicted seated before her mausoleum in Yarkand. The several traditional Uyghur musical instruments—12 total, to represent the number of muqams.

Abd al-Rashid, the mighty ruler of ***East Turkestan,*** wandered through a village, visiting some rural families while longing for His fancy urban home. As he sat with a local respected elder, he probably started to nod off. ***He heard a sweet, singsong voice recite a ghazal, a short rhyming poem.*** The words gripped him and cleared his mind—for the first time in his trip he was fully present and awake. ***"Did you write that?"*** he asked the shy daughter of the local elder. ***"Yes,"*** she said softly.
"Prove it!" he demanded in disbelief.
She composed another piece of equal quality on the spot. ***Overwhelmed by the talent before him, and the sheer beauty of her words, Abd al-Rashid proposed marriage with the same level of spontaneity.***

Amannisa Khan became a princess, but even more than her contributions to the just rule of the land, she is known for her composing and collecting verses. She brought together the musical pieces of her homeland, and, according to legend, **she preserved the twelve muqams.** *The Muqams are massive poetic musical collections that talk about loving Allah, tell funny stories, and so much more.* They are performed with many different Uyghur instruments. In the oldest history book that mentions Amannisa Khan, it is written, ***"She was peerless among the poets of the age and compiled a sweet book called Dīvān-i Nafīsī. She was an excellent calligrapher, and so perfect in music that the Sultan fell hopelessly in love with her."***

Amannisa Khan was an Uyghur, a member of a Muslim ethnic group native to East Turkestan. Her homeland was conquered by China centuries later, and is now referred to on most maps and in the news as *Xinjiang. Today, China is actively persecuting the Uyghurs—placing them and other Muslims in concentration camps, and working to destroy their faith and culture.* **Amannisa Khan shows how incredibly rich that culture is, and how integral it is to our collective history.**

Lessons:

- Amannisa Khan ***didn't compose poetry to impress anybody—but others still recognized how amazing it was.*** *Don't do things so others will praise them, do them because they will make Allah and you happy.*
- Amannisa Khan made it a point to preserve the history and culture of her people by collecting the twelve muqams. Uyghur tradition, like all other Muslim cultural traditions, contains its own unique and beautiful ways of pondering God and experiencing His creation. She recognized the inherent value in that tradition, and in history in general.

exer

1 **Adapt Shajar al-Durr's story into a fairy tale!** You can write it, draw it, or even just tell it to a friend. What themes will you emphasize in addition to relying on Allah? How does your fairy tale differ from typical fairy tales?

2 **Queen Amina was innovative and inventive.** So it's time for you to be an inventor! **Draw and/or write about an invention that would help Muslims!** What is it and how would it work? Is it a self-tying hijab, or a wudu machine, or something even cooler?

3 **Queen Amina worked hard to build and protect the roads, to make easy for people to travel, trade, and meet. Make a map of your own imaginary city, and include roads to bring as many people together as possible**! What does it look like?

4 **It's time for you to be a scholar and writer! Write at least one page reflecting on faith.** You can talk about love of God, you can write about any story from the life of the Prophet ﷺ, whatever you want. Who knows, this could be the start of your own 20+ books.

5 **A'isha traveled for knowledge.** When was the last time you traveled? When was the last time your learned something while traveling? **On your next trip out of town visit both a museum and a library in whichever place you're going to.**

cise

6 **Amannisa Khan made up her second Ghazal on the spot, with no preparation.** *She grabbed whatever inspiration she could find in the moment and ran with it. Sometimes creativity takes a lot of time, but a fear of starting and delaying creating as a result is often the largest obstacle to creative success.* **So, in the spirit of Amannisa Khan, write a ghazali right now with no practice and no erasing lines!** *A ghazal is at least 5 couplets one after another; if you can't make each couplet rhyme on the fly, that's okay, just write. Your topic can be anything.*

7 Amannisa Khan knew her culture really well and did her best to learn from it. What is your culture (or cultures)? What good aspects are there in it? What can you learn from it and share with others? If you don't know much about your culture, or you feel disconnected from it, how can you correct that?

Mihrimah Sultan

d. 1578
Istanbul, Turkey

Her Farsi name means "sun and moon,"
A Princess born with silver spoons.
But rather than enjoy the wealth,
She looks out for the kingdom's health.

In this illustration, Mihrimah is holding Mihrimah camii in Edirnekapi, in the same way that old Byzantine emperors are shown in mosaic artwork holding constructions they endowed. Mihrimah Sultan Camii in Uskudar is depicted in the green background.

When people hear your name, what is the first thing that comes to mind? A color, a feeling, or maybe a place? When people hear Mihrimah's name they think of two of the most beautiful mosques in Istanbul, which not only share her name—but were named in her honor and built due to her sponsorship. **Their soaring domes and sky-piercing minarets resonate with the melodic call to prayer.** One sits by an ancient city wall, the other in sight of the sea, but both mosques are filled with worshippers on a daily basis.

Mihrimah, *"the sun and moon"* of the Ottoman empire, was ***the daughter of Sultan Suleyman.*** **The princess was a powerful force in the royal household for decades, acting as an advisor for many rulers including her father, brother, and a vizier.** She was also known for being incredibly **charitable. She shaped the city of Istanbul like few others ever have.** She sponsored the building of two mosque complexes—***Mihrimah Sultan Camii in Uskudar*** and ***Mihrimah Camii in Edirnekapi.*** **These mosque complexes didn't just have places to pray, but also included schools, food pantries, guesthouses, and more.** She also commissioned the building of two more mosques on behalf of others—***Sinan Camii in Besiktas,*** and ***Rustem Pasha Camii in Eminonu.*** All of these mosques are still busy today, almost 500 years later. The deed of one of the mosques described Mihrimah as ***"a Fatima in innocence, a Khadija in purity, an A'isha in intelligence, a Bilqis (Queen of Sheba) in natural disposition," and "the Rabi'a of the epoch."***

Lessons:

-The Prophet ﷺ said, ***"Whoever builds a mosque, desiring thereby Allah's pleasure, Allah builds for him the like of it in paradise."*** **Mihrimah must have multiple palaces in paradise then!** Her concepts for the mosques weren't just about praying though—**her vision was broad.** ***Mosques were places of prayer, education, community gathering, and service to weak and ill.***

-Mihrimah had a lot of wealth and social status, ***but she didn't use it to party or be the most fashionable person in the room.*** **She used it in service of her hereafter and the people.**

Malahayati

d. 1615
Aceh province, Indonesia

She learns the din and its defense,
She goes to sea where things are tense.
She battles all colonialists,
She never stops, she balls her fists.

In this illustration, Malahayati leads a naval expedition. Her studious background is indicated by the books tangled with her hijab.

What stories do the sea winds whisper? What tales do the waters tell?

I imagine Malahayati's legend is one of their favorites. **She got her sea legs early in life, learning to swim and sail around her island home.** She wasn't given the time to make sand castles though, or listen to the soft sounds of shells. ***The tide brought in food and riches, but it also let in storms.*** Dutch and Portuguese sailors cast their anchors on ***Sumatra***'s shores, ***and sought to take what wasn't theirs, to conquer, pillage, and colonize.***

Her people were in danger. The sea called to her. She took the helm to save them all.

Malahayati became **the chief admiral—sea captain—**of the ***Sultanate of Aceh.*** **She defeated the Dutch in fight after fight, drowning their wicked ambitions with her fierce resolve.** She was lauded as a **hero** by her people during her lifetime, but being a hero wasn't enough for her—**she wanted to make others heros too.** ***She gathered together widows whose husbands were killed by the colonizers and trained them to fight back.***

Lessons:

- Malahayati, like Nusaybah before her, **put her life on the line to defend her people and faith.** She didn't just encourage good and forbid evil, ***she was the good.***

Malahayati didn't just defend her people—***she helped them to defend themselves.*** **That's true leadership—not to just be the one everyone depends on, but to make everyone around you dependable.**

Jahanara Begum

d. 1681
Delhi, India

She plays some polo, wins at chess,
While cleaning up the empire's mess.
She writes a book on Sufi saints,
From awe of God alone she faints.

In this illustration, Jehanara Begum is depicted standing in front of the Jasmine Tower in Agra, which was one of her favorite locations in which to write.

The Queen is the most powerful piece in the game of chess. She can move as many spaces as she pleases, **in any direction she desires.** Though she begins the game sheltered, hiding behind a line of pawns, she darts forward into danger with a strength no ordinary piece can manage. ***Jahanara Begum, a princess of the Mughal empire who was skilled at both chess and politics, knew the power of female royalty firsthand.*** And while she used her considerable intelligence to watch over the empire, she is best known for employing her substantial worldly means in the pursuit of the next world. ***Her free spiritual movement went in directions and levels that bring the chess board's Queen to shame.***

Jahanara Begum was the daughter of ***Shah Jahan,*** the ***Mughal Sultan*** who commissioned the building of the ***Taj Mahal.*** **She was active in the politics of the Empire, gave freely in charity, and had great success in business, but she is remembered most of all for being a spiritual devotee and master.** She authored books about the lives of walis ('friends of God' or 'saints') and on occasion, even wrote a little bit about **her own religious experiences**. She talked about being 'annihilated'—**erasing her ego, that constant "me, me, me" tendency, so that only God remains,** and she did her best to make that state of being a reality for her. The inscription on her grave reads, ***"He (Allah) is the Living, the Sustaining. Let no one cover my grave except with greenery, for this very grass suffices as a tomb cover for the poor. The Annihilated faqir Lady Jahanara..."***

Lessons:

- Jahanara Begum collected stories about the lives of saintly figures, and wrote a book about them. ***She knew that learning about the lives of the pious is a big help in becoming more pious, and her work is an inspiration for this whole book!***
- Jahanara Begum managed **to have fun, be charitable, stay politically active, and remain involved in the world, while at the same time engaging in spiritual contemplation and working to tame her ego.** She balanced a life in this world with a desire for the next world, and a love for God and those he loves.

Iparhan

d. 1788
Kashgar, China-Occupied East Turkestan

The Qing king steals her for her smell,
She does not fall beneath his spell.
She fights for homeland, faith, and self,
She is no doll upon the shelf.

In this illustration, Iparhan is depicted standing bravely before the East Turkestan flag. Several famous structures in East Turkestan are added to the illustration. The flowers behind Iparhan symbolize her famous scent.

When people think of the terrors of the holocaust, ***Anne Frank's*** story often comes to mind. When people think of the civil rights movement, they think of ***Dr. Martin Luther King Jr.*** and ***Rosa Parks.*** **Sometimes individuals become emblems, symbols, of something beyond themselves, poignant exemplars of causes and events. They represent the suffering and freedom fighting of whole peoples.**

Iparhan is a symbol and representative of the ***Uyghur struggle,*** **but she was a person living a valiant, brave, but difficult life first.**

When she was a teenager in her hometown of ***Kashgar***, the Chinese Qing empire invaded, ***and the long struggle for Uyghur freedom began***. The Qing emperor was obsessed with ***Iparhan's beauty and enchanted with her mysterious natural fragrance—in the same way he was obsessed with her homeland's resources and wealth.*** **She was kidnapped and her country was conquered.** He wanted to control her, but she refused to be his puppet—and her people followed suit. She stood up for herself and for other Muslims, and lost her life in the process. ***Today she remains a popular symbol of Uyghur resistance against Chinese state oppression.***

Lessons:

- Iparhan **submitted to no one but Allah.** ***It didn't matter what pretty things she was offered,*** she would not listen to the man who kidnapped her and conquered her people.
- Iparhan **became a symbol for an entire struggle.** She was a martyr, but her example lives on and inspires to this day. Allah says in the Quran, ***"And do not say of those who are killed in Allah's cause that 'they are dead.' No, but they're alive! But you don't perceive it."*** 2:154

exer

1 Is there a mosque you go to regularly? Or a mosque you've been to only a few times but which is close by? **How can you improve the mosque—making it better for all worshippers?** Can you clean it? Can you help with the Sunday or Saturday school? Or maybe advocate for the expansion of the women's prayer space! Come up with a mosque project or way to serve, and follow through!

2 **Build your own little masjid!** If you have space in your room, or somewhere outside, set up a prayer rug, or a sheet, or anything to keep the ground clean! Add decorations—draw your own calligraphy, or paint your own mosque. And then when its ready—pray! The Prophet ﷺ says that the whole earth is a masjid—a place of prostration and prayer. Show how that is so!

3 Malahayati loved the nature around her and used it in her defense against invaders. **Do we have the same appreciation for your environments, the same love and care?** Find a local bit of wildlife, a beach, or forest, or mountain, whatever happens to be around, and visit it! Think of Malahayati and her love of the ocean, and make tasbeeh as you walk around.

4 The ocean today is in great danger. People have tossed so much trash into it, that now there are whole islands of trash in some places and lots of fish and birds are hurt. Malahayati would be furious! **If there is a local body of water where you live, go pick up the trash there! And look into efforts to help clean the ocean.**

cise

5. Jahanara Begum enjoyed Chess, but she also used the skills she had for the game in her real life political maneuvering. **What's a game or board game that you enjoy?** What lessons can you extract from it that might help you in life—in your religious activity, school work, etc. Imam Ali said that **all knowledge is the property of the believer; even in fun situations we can learn a lot!**

6. Jahanara Begum wrote about pious, saintly people. **Who is someone you know, or someone you've heard of, who is close to God and inspirational?** They don't have to be famous. Write what you know about their story, and describe what kind of person they are. What good things can you learn from them?

7. The oppression that Iparhan experienced is ongoing today. Muslims in China are being put in concentration camps! **How can you help Uyghur Muslims and other Muslims who are being persecuted today?** Look up places you can donate, events you can attend, and other ways you can raise awareness or make a difference! Saveuighur.org is a great place to start.

Nana Asma'u

d. 1864
Sokoto, Nigeria

She teaches girls and ladies too,
So many learn from just a few.
Islam becomes accessible,
In every tongue addressable.

In her first major book she wrote, ***"Love for the Muslim community [is] shown by working for its best interests..."*** She worked for the community's best interests and showed incredible love.

In this illustration, Nana Asma'u is shown teaching women about Islam. Flowers sprout into the future from her efforts.

"And among His signs is the creation of the heavens and earth, and the diversity of your languages and colors. There truly are signs in this for those who know."—Qur'an 30:22

Arabic is the language of the Qur'an, and of the Prophet ﷺ, and it occupies a special place in our scholarly tradition. But, as Allah says, **languages in general are signs—not just Arabic. Every language is a unique path to praise and contemplate God.** The spread of Islam involved not only the spread of original sources, but the translation of the message into other tongues, and the production of knowledge and literature in them. ***Speaking to someone in their own language is how one reaches both their heart and mind, and Islam speaks to all levels of understanding.***

Nana Asma'u knew this better than almost anyone, **and she always spoke to the heart, mind, and soul.** Asma'u belonged to a famous ***Fulani*** family in ***West Africa.*** Her father, ***Uthman dan Fodio,*** founded the Sokoto Caliphate and promoted religious learning. **Growing up, she received the best education and showed the utmost dedication to her faith. She learned many languages and became a scholar, historian, poet, and teacher.** One of her relatives wrote, ***"She is marked by wisdom and kind deeds; her knowledge is like the wide sea."*** She did everything she could to make this knowledge accessible, and to expand it.

In her writing and teaching she made it a point to use **local languages** like Hausa and Fulani (and not just Arabic) so that everyone could understand and learn. She went beyond mere transmission, and trained other teachers, ***starting a massive women's education movement which cut across social divides.***

Lessons:

- Nana Asama'u didn't look down on people for speaking certain languages and not others. Instead, she followed the saying of Imam Ali RA, **"Speak to people according to their understanding."** She met people where they were at, ***and then brought them to new horizons***.
- Nana Asama'u didn't just teach—**she started a women's education movement!** ***She thought institutionally, she thought about the future, she thought about how to create a whole movement for change rather than just to enact change individually.***

Cut Nyak Dhien

d. 1908
Aceh Province, Indonesia

They rip her people's roots apart;
She claims the woods and fights with heart.
Her eyes go bad, her limbs are sore,
But still she looks and strives for more.

In this illustration, Cut Nyak Dhien is depicted based off of a photograph. The tan portion of the image is an approximation of the shape of the island of Sumatra in which Aceh is located. Her hands are rooted in her homeland, showing her dedication to it.

Cut Nyak Dhien lived a charmed life, she had everything—and then one day, everything was gone. **She was raised in wealth and happiness, she received a well-rounded religious education, she had a loving marriage and a peaceful life.** ***And then the Dutch attacked.***

In the beginning, she sought safety with other women, taking cover as her husband fought. But when he was killed, years after the fighting began, she had enough. *She took up the blade and entered the battle—and became a legend.* She took refuge in the lush jungle, ***in its tangle of humming and buzzing life,*** and began her famous resistance. ***The Dutch did not know the land they were trying to steal; she made them pay for the attempt.***

When her second husband Umar, another freedom fighter, sought her hand in marriage, **she only agreed when she was sure she would still be able to keep the campaign going.** The two pulled off a series of daring exploits, and when he was tragically killed, she led the rebel army—even after starting to go blind. She was finally captured by the Dutch and exiled, but her daughter escaped and the struggle continued.

Lessons:

- Like Malahayati before her, Cut Nyak Dhien **witnessed evil**—the invasion of her home—**and worked to change it with her hands,** following the hadith of the Prophet ﷺ. ***She was a literal hero.***
- Cut Nyak Dhien **never lost hope in God. *She went blind,*** but still she **fought** and **strategized**. She was removed from the fighting, but her daughter kept her legacy alive. ***No matter how dark the future might have seemed, she knew that God is capable of changing it and we must never give up.***

Fatima bt. Abdullah

d. 1912
Tripoli, Libya

When raiders come with the hot sun,
She testifies that God is one.
Defender's lips are parched and dry,
She gives them water like the sky.

In this illustration, Fatima is depicted giving water to soldiers, and shielding her people from bullets.

The Prophet ﷺ *compared giving a cup of water to freeing a slave;* by that measure, Fatima was submerged in **a sea of good deeds.**

She was only 11 years old when the Italians attacked her home; ***too young to hold a sword, too small to wage a war,*** **but her heart was too big for her to simply look on and do nothing.** *She went out into the field, bringing water for soldiers to sip.* The battle was heavy, the environment was hot; Fatima kept the defenders of her people going, bringing life to their dry veins, ***quenching their thirst and reviving their spirits.***

She was shot by an invader; a bullet put a tragic end to her young life, but she'd already done more in those few years than many do in lifetimes. ***Her stalwartness, bravery, and mercy were like water for Muslims far beyond her country's borders, all of whom were thirsty for hope and inspiration.***

The *famous* South Asian poet **Allama Iqbal** commemorated her bravery in moving verses that begin: *"Fatimah, you are the pride of the lost nation/Your dust is holy, every particle of it."*

Lessons:

- ***Fatimah was young and she wasn't rich or famous.*** But still she knew that through **the simple act of giving people water, she could help.** And so she did. **Sometimes the most seemingly small actions can make the biggest difference and be the most inspiring—and can be the most most loved by Allah.**

Begum Rokeya

d. 1932
Kolkata, West Bengal, India

She writes sci-fi before it's cool,
She sends a bunch of girls to school.
She goes debating for whole nights,
She fights all day for women's rights.

Near the end of "Sultana's Dream," the Queen of the fictional land in her story says what women there do and what Rokeya herself always did: "We dive deep into the ocean of knowledge and try to find out the precious gems, which nature has kept in store for us. We enjoy nature's gifts as much as we can."

In this illustration, Begum Rokeya stands with children before a vivid portrayal of a book showing some of the innovations she imagined in her story "Sultana's Dream."

Before Star Wars and Star Trek, there was Sultana's dream—**an evocative, detailed sci-fi story imagining a better world.** Begum Rokeya brought together her **love of words** with her considerable **creativity**, ***and crafted one of the first science fiction tales ever.***

In the story, she critiqued the difficult situation women faced in society and described a ***utopia***—an ideal world—run by them. She predicted ***solar energy*** and envisioned ***automated farming***, she talked about ***flying cars*** and ***weather balloons. She saw people living in high-tech harmony with the world, rather than exploiting or abusing it.***

In the words of G. B. Shaw, **she dreamed of things that never were, and asked, "*why not?*"**

Writing wasn't Begum Rokeya's only accomplishment; she also established an ***all-girls school*** and fought for ***women's fundamental right to vote and receive an education.***

Lessons:

- Begum Rokeya knew that **women's participation in society and increased education** were the keys to a bright future for women and society as a whole. She worked hard to reach those goals through ***writing, founding and funding institutions, and being an advocate.***
- Begum Rokeya worked to create a better future, but she also spent time **imagining** what that future might be. ***She didn't let words like "impossible" and "no way" get in her way!***

exer

1 Do you know any languages besides English? It's okay if not! **Try making dua in every language you know, and if you know just one language, ask friends and teachers how to make dua in their languages. Try to make dua in every language that you can!** How did it feel? Allah hears and knows all languages, and each is a unique and beautiful path to call on him through.

2 What sort of movement would you found? What's an issue that you think needs to be addressed, what sort of change do you wish to see? Write a name for your movement and jot down a list of things it would do and how!

3 How is your eyesight? If you can see, thank Allah for it, and then close your eyes. **Try to walk around—in a safe, obstacle free environment—with your eyes closed.** What was it like for Cut Nyak Dhien to navigate leadership with little sight? If you don't have good sight or can't see at all, thank Allah for what he's given you and make dua for perfect perception in the next life.

4 Malahayati loved her homeland and worked to protect it. **What do you love about where you are from? How can you protect those aspects of your homeland? What do you not like about where you are from?** Brainstorm ways to make it better—those are ways to protect it too! Many people today claim that they support their country "right or wrong." The politician Carl Schurz corrected that idea—he said **"My country, right or wrong; if right, to be kept right; and if wrong, to be set right."** The Prophet ﷺ summed up the same idea on a more basic, universal level. He said **"Help your brother, wheth-**

cise

er he is an oppressor or he is an oppressed one." The people asked, "O Allah's Apostle! It is all right to help him if he is oppressed, but how should we help him if he is an oppressor?" The Prophet said, **"By preventing him from oppressing others."**

5 The Prophet ﷺ called giving water the best charity. **Its an easy Sunnah to fulfill and a great way to honor Fatimah's legacy!** At the next meal you attend, pour water for everyone at the table. If you leave home with a water bottle, keep an extra one with you and hand it to someone who seems thirsty.

6 **Begum Rokeya wrote Sci-fi—now it's your turn!** Imagine a future that you want to happen. A future with Islam, and peace, and whatever else you find wholesome and inspiring. Write a description of this 'utopic' future, or draw it!

7 Begum Rokeya fought for women's rights! What's a right that people are being deprived of today, or what's something they're forced to do that they shouldn't have to do. **How can you be an advocate like Begum Rokeya?**

Zaynab Fawaz

D. 1914
Tebnine, Lebanon & Alexandria, Egypt

This playwright brings a tale to life,
With faith and hope, she guides its flight.
She speaks of women from the past,
And writes so that their stories last.

In an essay on the importance of charity published in Egypt, she wrote: ***"And you, women of the East, and Egyptian women specifically, give priority to this virtuous action (charity). I do not say: [Simply] donate. I say: Commence doing the work you ought to do, forming societies, collecting money..."***

In this illustration, Zaynab Fawwaz is depicted based on a famous photograph of her. The various women added to her fan reference her work documenting the lives of influential women in history.

Zaynab was a small-town girl; she probably grew up with the bleating of goats and the wafting smells of fertilizer. With a bit of pluck and spunk, she got a job as a maid in a palace, dusting off decorations and making beds.

In Good Will Hunting Fashion, this janitor's genius was soon discovered. She started taking lessons with the prince's wife and soon began surprising and surpassing her patron with her writing prowess. She moved to Egypt where she continued to study and wrote about women's issues for magazines and newspapers. She argued in her articles that women should not be stuck at home and that women are equal to men.

She authored a massive book on women in history because she saw a lack of works written about ***"half the human world"***—it has far more entries than this short book. She also wrote two novels and was the first Arab woman to be a playwright. Her life was as inspiring as that of the heroines from her own stories.

Lessons:

- Like Jahanara Begun, Zaynab's writing inspires this book! She wrote way more women's biographies with far more depth.
- ***She knew the power of storytelling and sharing the examples of others, but she didn't know that her life story and her example would also become so incredible.***

Fatma Aliye

d. 1936
Istanbul, Turkey

A well-known Turkish novelist
She heads so many author lists!
She starts a women's charity.
Her skill is such a rarity.

Fatma wrote, *"...in matters of humanity, there is no difference between women and men. We are all human beings."*

In this illustration, Fatma is shown writing one of her books on a typewriter. An istanbul cat sits on the bookshelf beside.

When someone is the subject of an entire biography—a whole book about their life—it usually means they accomplished a lot. *They transformed the way we think, or acted as an incredible role model. The first biography about Fatma Aliye was written during her life...* **when she was only 33!** *That says volumes about the breakneck, fast pace at which she was living.*

Fatma was the daughter of one of the Ottoman empire's leading intellectuals, but she paved her own path to fame. She was one of the first Muslim women and Turkish novelists ever! She also translated works from French, published articles, and wrote an essay on women in Islam. She started a charity to help soldiers' families, and was a member of the humanitarian organization known as "the Ottoman Red Crescent." She told intense, dramatic stories but lived a life that made them dull in comparison.

Lessons:

- **Fatma told stories, not just to entertain but also to make people think and convey the social and political realities of her time.** She used her writing talents to reach hundreds of thousands of people—to this day!
- Fatma didn't let herself be boxed in as one thing. She was a novelist AND a scholar, a philanthropist AND an activist. If there was any way she could use her skills to benefit society, she would try it out. **She didn't just stick to what was comfortable—she constantly evolved in her quest to prove and protect the humanity of Muslim women.**

Mukhlisa Bubi

d. 1937
Kazan, Tatarstan, Russia

Sincere means honest, true, and pure—
That word defines this judge for sure.
She never settles for a truce,
when guarding women from abuse!

In her speech at the opening of a girl's school in 1914, Mukhlisa said, *"the most important thing for the happiness and preservation of our nation and the most necessary thing for strengthening our religion is educating our women and adorning them with knowledge."*

In this illustration, Mukhlisa Bubi is depicted based on a photograph. The structure in the background is Söyembikä Tower, a major landmark in Kazan.

Who deliberates and decides what to do when neighbors have a dispute? Who sentences criminals to their sentences and advises on business contracts? In Islamic history, the ruler might do some of this, but on the local level, the representative of justice, the paragon of Islamic education, was the Qadi—the judge. With a social and political role well beyond what the translation might suggest today, becoming a Qadi was a huge deal. And the first female Qadi in the present era was none other than Mukhlisa Bubi. She didn't bask in her authority or have fun with it, but instead used it always to protect the less fortunate. Mukhlisa was from the vibrant city of Kazan, formerly the stronghold of a Muslim Khanate but by her time, a piece of the Russian empire. She was a scholar and educator who lived her sense of justice and made her visions of equality real. She was active in religious renewal movements and believed that Muslim women should be educated, so she founded a modern all-girls school. On May 11, 1917, she was elected as Qadi. She used her status to fight for women's rights and protect women in their marriages. The then-communist regime eventually cracked down on the practice of Islam, and Mukhlisa, too devout and empowered for their tastes, was martyred by them in 1937. Her name means sincere in Arabic, and that describes her character perfectly.

Lessons:

-Religious sciences, law, and justice are the domain of women as much as they are of men. By being the first Female Qadi in the present era, Mukhlisa proved this.

-Mukhlisa fought for the rights of Muslim women using the political and social system she lived in, using elections and education to further her cause. Unfortunately the government turned against her, but she did her best with whatever means were available to her, and died a martyr.

Lady Zainab Cobbold

d. 1963
Edinburgh & Inverness, Scotland, UK

The light of faith is in her heart,
Acceptance brings a brand new start.
She goes for Hajj to clean her slate,
To write and travel is her fate.

Zainab begins her famed book with the following passage. ***"I am often asked when and why I became a [Muslim]. I can only reply that I do not know the precise moment when the truth of Islam dawned on me. It seems that I have always been a Moslem. This is not so strange when one remembers that Islam is the natural religion that a child left to itself would develop. Indeed, as a western critic once described it, 'Islam is the religion of common sense.'"***

In this illustration, Lady Zainab is depicted with an excerpt of her travelogue behind her. The basic route of her journey, from Scotland to the Kaaba is shown on her clothes. The Kaaba is on her heart, because the journey to Allah's house is also a trip to her heart's home.

At some point when she was a young woman, the Scottish noble Lady Evelyn was staying in Rome with some Italian friends. She got the exciting news one day that she would get to meet the pope—the head of the catholic church himself! She dressed in black clothes and wearing a long veil, she stepped nervously into his presence. He asked her innocently, "Are you catholic?"

She paused for a moment. "I'm Muslim," she said slowly. And she had no idea why she'd answered that way. She'd never converted to Islam, and had barely read anything about it. Though she had spent time in Muslim countries in North Africa, she hadn't thought much about her experiences there.

She decided to read about Islam, and soon found that she had really been a Muslim at heart for a long time without knowing it. She converted and took the name Zainab. In 1933, she became the first British woman to go for Hajj! She proceeded to write her famed account of her journey, recording both her own observations and many historical anecdotes. She ends her book with the reflection, "to me an amazing new world had been revealed." And she in turn revealed the amazing world of her learning and experiences to us.

Lessons:

- Converting to Islam means changing one's life. It is being so committed to faith that one is willing to face rejection by family and friends. Zainab didn't experience that rejection, and she felt that her life changed little because she was already so Muslim in spirit. Still, her willingness to risk rejection and her wholehearted attachment to faith is inspiring.

-Zainab traveled for hajj and learned and experienced so much from the journey that she wrote a book! Travel is a transformative experience and the hajj is one of the pillars of faith!

exer

1 Like Zaynab Fawaz, write a few accounts describing what girls and women do that impresses you and why.

2 A biography was written about Fatma Aliye when she was pretty young. It's got to make you wonder—how did hearing her own life story affect her going forward? Did it inspire her? Increase her resolve to do more? Write your own autobiography! It can be a paragraph, or pages. Look at what you've done in life, reflect on it, and then think about how you can improve and do more!

3 Fatma was a novelist and storyteller. The stories she wrote were often fiction, but that didn't stop them from holding deeper truths. Write a short fiction story, but make sure it has a message! Get your creative juices flowing.

4 Mukhlisa involved herself in modern politics. Are there any political issues in your society that you support or have strong opinions on as a Muslim? How can you get involved in making a difference like Mukhlisa? Write up a plan and work with you parents, friends, and mentors to make it a reality!

cise

5 Mukhlisa was a judge, who thought deeply and researched heavily when making all of her decisions. Imagine what it would be like to be a judge, in fact; draw yourself as a judge! What would your judgements be based on? What principles would you follow? Write them down!

6 **Zainab wrote about why she was Muslim! Why are you Muslim? Write a page giving all your reasons and all the circumstances that made you and make you Muslim!**

7 Zainab wrote about a journey. What's a trip that you have taken recently? Draw a map and highlight the route you took. List all the things that happened on the trip and what you learned from them!

Shaykha Maimouna al-Kabir

d. 20th century
Touba, Senegal

This hafiz holds the word of God,
It makes her heart a lightning rod.
She's filled with fierce electric faith,
And writes Qur'ans without a break.

In this illustration, Maimouna is depicted based on an actual photogram of her. The lightning and books are an addition signifying her learning and electrifying connection to the Qur'an.

How much of the Qur'an have you memorized? How many Huffaz do you know? It's not an easy task, to remember every word and recite it flawlessly. It's even harder to embody what the text says—to live it out and to be a "walking Qur'an."

Few people had a connection to the text like Maimouna al-Kabir. She didn't just memorize Allah's word—she wrote the whole thing out, twenty times, by heart! Each copy would have taken hundreds of hours. She also didn't just follow the Qur'an's message—she made it her every breath, and became one of Senegal's most famous emblems of piety.

Maimouna was the daughter of Shaykh Ahmadou Bamba, one of the most renowned Sufi leaders of Senegal. She too was a scholar and spiritual master, a stand-out, even in her illustrious family. She stood as an example of piety for many who dealt with the harsh realities of French colonization and inspires Muslims in Senegal and around the world to this day.

Lessons:

-The Qur'an is at the center of our faith and civilization. It is the foundation for our law, our beliefs, and reciting it is our primary way of understanding God and a major way we connect to Him. History books, geography works, stories collections—they would all start by quoting a verse. Major events in peoples' lives across the world, simple moments in our daily existence, they all supplemented by Surahs. Maimouna recognized the importance of the Quran and gave her life to it, and so her life was illuminated. She knew it was revelation from God, and therefore she treated it with reverence and love.

Mother Khadijah Faisal

d. 1992
Bermuda & Brooklyn, NY, USA

In Brooklyn's soil, she plants a seed,
And waters it with word and deed.
A place of prayer blossoms now,
where people gather, saying wow.

The painting is based partially on a photograph of Khadijah. The Islamic Mission of America/Masjid Dawood is located at 143 State St, Brooklyn, NY 11201. In this illustration, Mother Khadijah is depicted in front her mosque, metaphorically gardening and nurturing her community.

The word mother implies care and concern, the strength and willingness to nurture, the ability to teach, and inspire. Khadijah Faisal was called mother by the members of her community because she brought them together, cared for them, and shaped them into something more than they were.

Khadijah was born on the Caribbean island of Bermuda. As a young adult, she moved to New York City and pursued a career combining the arts and education. She was a brilliant singer, but even better at tuning into the sounds of people's souls. She dedicated her life to ensuring the spiritual and cultural growth of others. In 1939, she and her husband turned their own home into a Brooklyn mosque for this purpose.

It became a renowned center for Islamic learning and immigrant advocacy, a place for both religious practice and community work. Khadijah's work didn't stop at the doors of the mosque—she remained a part of New York's arts scene where she showcased the musical traditions of Muslim cultures. She also headed the Muslim Ladies Cultural Society and mentored younger women.

Lessons:

-Building a masjid is a sadiqa jariya—a charity that lasts after death and keeps benefiting the donor! Khadijah and her husband gave an incredible sadiqa jariya. But more than just create a place to pray, they created a space for community. Being Muslim, especially in minority situations—but really everywhere, isn't something that is easy to do alone. Having friends and mentors, brothers and sisters in faith, is important. Mother Khadijah created that family-like, communal setting, following the Prophet ﷺ's own example.

Betty Shabbaz

d. 1997
New York, NY, USA

Six kids to feed, a husband killed,
But still she finds the strength to build.
She goes and gets her PhD,
For freedom's fight, the mind is key.

Betty Shabbaz once prayed, ***"I wish you power that equals your intelligence and your strength. I wish you success that equals your talent and determination. And I wish you faith."*** That prayer came true first for herself.

In this illustration, Betty Shabbaz is depicted with her six children. She has her PhD, the legacy of her husband, and everlasting values of freedom and justice.

It's easy to do the right things and make a difference when things are going well. It's when everything goes wrong, and a person must react, however, that their true character is shown. Betty Shabbaz faced tragic, harsh circumstances—the brutal murder of her loving husband, and life as a single in a racist society. She proved that her character and resolve were astounding.

Betty Shabbaz went to college in the South, where segregation plagued the lives of African Americans. Black people could not swim in the same pools as white people, could not live in the same developments, or drink from the same water fountains. Being lynched and killed by a white mob was a real and present fear. Betty thought she escaped the dangerous south when she moved to New York to study nursing. She quickly found that there, the racism was more polite, but no less present. After a few years, she joined the Nation of Islam, a movement drawing from the Islamic tradition which promoted sentiments of communal strength and independence. She married the Nation's star preacher, Malcolm X. She supported him in all his activism, despite the risks she faced, and joined him in embracing Islam near the end of his life. When he was assassinated in 1965, she was left with their four kids, and was pregnant with twins. She struggled to make ends meet, but with the aid of friends, prayers, and a lot of striving, she managed to take care of her children and complete her PhD. She became a professor and later an administrator at Medgar Evers College while also serving as an activist in her own right, bringing together and inspiring a new generation. Her commitment to education forms the foundation for the Shabazz center today.

Her longtime friend Eleanor Holmes Norton, remarked, "Many would have been satisfied to have been the wife of a great man who was assassinated. What people forget is that many great men married great women."

Lessons:

-Betty faced a profound loss. There is nothing wrong with feeling grief or with experiencing depression. The Prophet ﷺ himself cried when he lost a child, and he called the year when Khadijah رضي الله عنها passed away the year of sorrow. But Betty and the Prophet both didn't condemn God for their misfortune; instead they worked for futures their loved ones would have loved.

-Betty had a career and had a family. Being a professional and being a mother are both incredible goals; Betty showed that doing both at the highest, most impressive levels is possible. Her faith and intellect were always apparent in both her home life and work.

Zainab Asvat & Amina Chachalia

d. 2013
Johannesburg, South Africa

These sisters march for something more:
An end to walls, an even score.
Though thrown in jail or forced to flee-
They struggle on till all are free!

When Zainab was pushed by racists attacking her and the protesters with her, she said, "It's not their fault, they don't know what they are doing" and "Hooligans or no hooligans, carry on we must, and carry on we shall."

In this illustration, the sisters are depicted based on a photograph. The varieties of palm trees in the background are common in South Africa.

A black man is arrested for talking to a white kid in a white neighborhood. A brown family can only live in certain sections of town. An interracial couple walk seperate from each other, on opposite sides of the street so as not to draw attention.

These are examples of Apartheid, a system of segregation, discrimination, and institutionalized racism practiced for decades in South Africa. Zainab and Amina were sisters who grew up under this system; they lived as second class citizens, but many in their 'racial classification' accepted the status quo—the way things were—because they experienced less difficulties than the black population. Zainab and Amina would not stand for any inequality—whether or not it hurt them. They took seriously the verse in the Qur'an, "stand for justice, even if it is against your own selves."

Zainab trained as a doctor and joined the Passive Resistance Campaign against Apartheid. She joined protests and marches, and helped other activists when they were taken to court. She was placed under house arrest so many times that she and her husband finally left the country. Amina, the younger of the two siblings, handed out leaflets talking about the injustices of apartheid and even aided activists in escaping prison. She also helped organize a women's march that had 20,000+ attendees. She later fought against government efforts to break Indian and black African solidarity. After Apartheid, she was elected to parliment under the new government. She wrote an autobiography with the title, "When Hope and History Rhyme."

Lessons:

-Zainab and Amina risked their lives and abandoned their comfort to struggle for justice. Al-Adl, the Just, is a name of Allah, and they worked to live that name. Muslim rulers throughout history, political manuals, hadith, and the quran itself—all preach justice is one of the cheif virtues of Islam, alongside mercy. Zainab and Amina were clearly aware of that.

-Zainab and Amina used whatever means were available to them to further fight against apartheid. This included passing out leaflets, participating in and organizing marches and protests, and so on. Struggling for justice doesn't have to be fancy—simple things like being present and chanting together to raise awareness of a situation can go a long way.

exer

1 One of the ways Maimouna demonstrated her love of the Qur'an and practiced her memorization, was by writing it! Have you ever written down a verse from the Quran before? If not, now is a good time to try! You might not be able to write the Arabic letters, that's okay though—trace and ask for help from a teacher. How did it feel to write a verse down? If you need to dispose of what you wrote, remember to ask a parent for help because things with words from the Quran on them can't be tossed into the trash. Here is a sample verse if you are having trouble picking one!
"Indeed with hardship comes ease." 94:6. Allah gives ease after difficulty, and always ultimately replenishes us!

2 Masjids are places of prayer and community. They don't grow spontaneously out of the ground—they're built! Some have centuries of history, and others were finished yesterday. Some were sponsored by princesses, and others were funded by working class folks. Is there a mosque near you? Have you spent time there? Look into its history and write about it! What lessons can you learn from the example of the folks who made it?

3 Khadijah's masjid has an active community to this day where both men and women feel welcome and fulfilled. Unfortunately that's not true for every Muslim community or every mosque. Sometimes women's prayer spaces are the size of a closet and have no AC. Thats not right! Everyone deserves to pray in peace and comfort. How would you design your own mosque? What changes would you make to your local mosque? Draw it out and write down some ideas!

c i s e

4 Much of Betty's life work involved fighting against racism. She and her husband saw the crimes against African Americans not just as civil rights issues but human rights issues. Have you experienced or noticed racism? Especially if you just witnessed it, did you speak out against it?

5 Amina distributed leaflets—informational pamphlets—which talked about the injustice in her society. Acts as simple as passing out leaflets and making them made a difference! Make your own leaflet documenting injustices in YOUR society. Turn a paper horizontally and fold it into three parts, then fill each with words and drawings explaining things that are wrong in society. Make dua for justice, and note down possible solutions to the injustices you've noticed on the other side of the paper!

6 Both Amina and Zainab participated in marches and protests! Find a protest for an issue you support—a protest for Palestine, or for Rohingya human rights, for example. Attend the protest with a parent or guardian, and write a paragraph explaining what it was like!

Bilquis Edhi

d. 2022
Karachi, Pakistan

She hears the cries of little kids,
And finds them under basket lids.
She wipes their tears with old white sheets,
And saves the lives of all she meets.

Referring to the many kids she has cared for, she said. ***"I love that these children call me ammi (mother)."***

In this illustration, Bilquis Edhi is depicted caring for orphaned children. She is surrounded by baskets like those in which people would abandon babies that she would rescue.

It was her wedding day—a moment she'd waited for, for ages. And yet on that happy day, rather than enjoy the celebration, Bilquis cared for an injured child, wrapping and soothing the kid's wounds with her skill and the warmth of her presence. That is the kind of person that Bilquis Edhi was—one who takes care of others, who lives to serve any and all who have been hurt.

Bilquis grew up in Karachi, Pakistan. As a teenager, she joined Pakistan's largest humanitarian and charity organization, the Edhi foundation, and trained as a nurse to serve the less fortunate. Abdul Sattar Edhi, the founder, was so impressed with her work and vision that one day he proposed to her. She eventually took charge of the foundation's child services projects, which include rescuing abandoned babies, taking care of them, and setting up adoptions. She helped save and serve as a mother figure to over 16,000 children, and worked well into her 70's! She passed away in April of 2022.

Rabia Bibi Osman, a baby who had been rescued by the Edhi foundation, wrote the following upon hearing the news of Bilquis' death. "28 years ago I was abandoned in a baby carriage at the Edhi Orphanage located in Karachi, Pakistan. You found me, you named me after your mother Rabia Bano, you forged my identity, and then you gave me a home. Because of you today... I am somebody, I have an identity, and I have loving parents to call my own."

Lessons:

-Bilquis Edhi, even on a day when she was supposed to party and relax, chose to serve. She lives a selfless life, giving not just money but also time and comfort up for the sake of others. Working for the sake of God and His creation rather than our own selves is hard because our egos are so strong, but Bilquis shows that it's possible to move past them.

-Bilquis, unlike Mihrimah, Razia, and others we read about earlier, didn't occupy a position of power which she used to help others. Rather, she pursued an education and chose a career that would allow her to serve others. Healthcare, which is Bilquis' specialty, is a great way to help others; doctors and nurses relieve pain, promote healing, and with the right intention, make God pleased. But healthcare isn't the only career that can serve others—engineering, nonprofit work, humanities—when done with the right intention and eye towards helping the ummah, almost any type of work can become something which pays dividends in the next life and not just this life.

Farkhondeh Sadegh, Laleh Keshavarz, and Leila Bahrami

Tehran, Iran

"At Everest our God is near"
His Majesty—through clouds—is clear.
These women climb the highest peak,
And find the wonder that they seek.

In that wondrous moment at the peak, Farkhondeh said,
"At Everest, God is near."

In this illustration, Laleh and Farkhondeh are shown on the peak of Everest while Leila, who is injured, sits not far below. The clouds at the top are in the shape of the word Allah written in arabic.

When people talk about achieving their goals and becoming successful, they often use the metaphor of ***"conquering the summit."*** That metaphor, of course, comes from climbing mountains. The literal 'highest summit' in the world is *Mount Everest*; its jagged peak tears into the sky **29,000** feet from the earth's surface. ***The first Muslim women to attempt the treacherous ascent to the top were Farkhondeh and Leila.***

They dreamed of climbing into the clouds for years, and with a team of their fellow Iranian countryfolk, they got the chance in 2005. Leila said in an interview, ***"As a mountaineer, I would like to do it as well as I can; on the other hand, I would like to do it for Muslim women...People often seem to think Muslim women are limited. It would be a good chance to show the world that something like this is possible for us."*** She was injured on the way up and didn't reach the peak, but Laleh, another member of the team, joined Farkhondeh at the top. There they sat in a state of complete awe as they beheld the revelation of God at the highest altitudes, in the rock and wind, and the jaw-dropping view.

Lessons:

- The world itself is a form of revelation. The experience of awe, of seeing something so transcedant it makes you say subhanAllah, is a way to affirm faith and is a religious experience that can be a form of worship. These women sought out and experienced wonder—which led them to think of God.
- Climbing Everest was an amazing accomplishment for these women, but they didn't just do it for themselves or for the fun of it. They did it to prove the capabilities of Muslim women—they did it to change impressions about other Muslim women and empower them . They were trailblazers and they were aware that they were trailblazers.

Burçin Mutlu-Pakdil

Istanbul, Turkey &
currently Chicago, IL, USA

She listens closely from afar,
To secrets whispered by each star.
She finds a type of galaxy,
And shows us all its majesty.

When talking about people in her life who discouraged her from a career in science or made her work difficult, she said, "If I tried to follow their path, I wouldn't be happy. This life is too short to follow other's views. So in the end, I said, "Nevermind, I don't care what you think about me. I am me. So I will live my life."

In this illustration, Burçin is depicted thinking of the heavens. The large double ringed structure is a model of what the galaxy she discovered may look like.

Burçin Mutlu-Pakdil **"studies the most peculiar objects in the universe."** Those objects are celestial—stars and planets out in space; Burçin is an astrophysicist who makes sense of the mysteries written in the night's sky.

Burçin grew up in Istanbul, a front-runner for being the "capital of the world," and moved to her country, Turkey's capital city, Ankara. There she began her educational journey to the top of the scientific world.

From the very beginning, her path was filled with obstacles; there was a discriminatory ban on headscarves in universities in Turkey at the time, and her school program had very few women. She writes that a professor told her, *"Are you crazy? You are a woman, and you left your hometown to study physics?"* She didn't let the criticism stop her; **she shot for the stars and reached them.**

She continued her career in Astrophysics in the US and with her team, discovered a unique double-ringed galaxy which expanded our knowledge of the universe.

Lessons:

- People doubted Burçin, they doubted the place of a Muslim woman in science. But she knew about the incredible woman before her, and she was ready to be an example and role model for all the women after her. ***It wasn't easy, but she studied and prayed hard, and literally made her mark in the sky!***

Grandmas

Al-Razi envies grandma's hope,
A Faith more pure than any soap.
She raised her kids and helps with theirs,
She shows us love and how to care.

Grandmas are the real foundation of society! They pass on generations of knowledge and wisdom, teach languages, preserve traditions, and dote on their grandkids. They're our first link to history and so often, to God. Grandmas are remarkable for their deep piety; Fakhr al-Din al-Razi, the famed 12th century Muslim theologian, once said,

"I wish I had the faith of an old woman."

May Allah bless all grandmas—
those who are with us,
and those who have passed away
into his grace.
Ameen.

exer

1 Have you saved up any money? Do you have any Eidee, or did you do a chore which got you paid? It's okay if you don't any, or if you only have a tiny amount. Give something to charity, however tiny—even if its a single penny or used socks. Philanthropy—charity work—is Bilquis' bread and butter and inshaallah now it's yours too! The Qur'an says that whatever you give in Allah's cause will be paid back seven-fold.

2 Are there any hills or mountains near where you live? If so, ask a parent/guardian if you can climb it together! Take all the precautions that you can. Recklessly endangering yourself is NOT part of Islam. Whats the view from the top like?

3 What's an experience of wonder, of total awe, that you've had? Draw or write about it! And then say SubhanAllah—"Glory be to Allah" (because Allah is amazing) as many times as you can!

4 Is there an observatory or planetarium near where you live? Look it up, and if so, go on a trip there with family and friends! Write about what you saw. How did it make you think about God? What scientific activity do you want to do next?

5 Write down a few things you love most about your grandmother—or someone else's granny. Put on a skit where you play-act being the way that these beloved grandmothers are! Then, think if you can be this way with people in daily life—even if you are so much younger! Tell us what happens!

c i s e

Draw yourself doing something you love to do. It can be a stick drawing. If, in Life, you keep on with what you love, you will one day notice you are always being drawn towards the special person who you really ARE *and the exact gift you are to deliver to this world!*

A Few of the Many Resilient Women of Gaza

Heba Zaghout

She paints bright skies and wizened trees.
She prays that Palestine be free.
An artist, dreamer, doting mom;
Her hope is greater than their bomb

Rouzan Al-Najjar

With splotched white coats and nerves of steel,
Rouzan goes out to help and heal.
When soldiers shoot, she's at the scene.
To seal the victim's wounds and clean.

Bisan Owda

She's taking pictures, showing life,
She shines amid the pain and strife.
Due to her fight for Gaza's youth,
The news can't cover up the truth.

Heba Zaghout *was an artist from Gaza. She captured the beauty and character of her homeland in her vibrant paintings. She raised two kids while sharing her wholesome pieces on social media. She was killed by an Israeli air strike on October 12, 2023.*

Rouzan al-Najjar *was a medic from Gaza. When Palestinian protestors were shot by IDF soldiers in 2018, she was a first responder. She braved bullets and brutality to save lives. She was targeted and killled by the IDF while trying to evacuate the wounded. She was only 21 years old.*

Bisan Owda *is a photographer and journalist from Gaza. She has actively shared what she and her people are going through amidst the current genocide. She has shown instances of joy despite the immense suffering, and has demonstrated more resilience than anyone should ever have to. She has called for global boycotts, and inspired activists worldwide.*

These are only three stories of Palestinian women affected by the Israeli occupation. For over 70 years at the time of this writing, Palestinians have faced persecution. It's up to us to stand with them and give them our support.

You

The fate of thousands starts with one;
The smallest light outshines the sun.
Go build on those who came before-
Each obstacle is just a door.

With His great grace, a path will clear,
There is no roof, success is near.
The coming lines are yours to write-
Allah will make the future bright.

. . . .
. . . .
. . . .
. . . .

We believe in you and can't wait to see what you achieve! May Allah bless your every step and inspire your every act. Go make your family, your friends, your foremothers, the ummah, and most importantly, Allah, proud.

Draw yourself here!